DEFENDING

DUI

Defense Strategies for DUI in Illinois

Second Edition

Jonathan E. James Esq.

LEGAL DISCLAIMER

This book is for general information purposes only. This book gives a general overview of criminal DUI prosecutions in Illinois. This book is not legal advice and is not intended to provide specific legal advice or instruction on any specific situation. Reading this book does not create an attorney-client relationship between you and attorney Jonathan James, or the Law Office of Jonathan James, LLC. This book is based entirely on Illinois law. You should always direct any specific questions you have about your case to your own lawyer. No lawyer (including the author of this book) can ever make you any promises or guarantees about how your case will turn out.

CHAPTER 1

INTRODUCTION

I'm glad you decided to purchase a copy of this book on DUI Defense Strategies in Illinois. This book can help you understand the options you have when facing DUI charges and what you should do to protect your rights and your license.

This book can help you answer many of the common questions you may have about a DUI charge:

- How serious is a DUI charge and what are the possible penalties?
- What will happen to my license if I'm charged with DUI?
- What if I wasn't driving?
- What if the police didn't read me my rights?
- If my BAC was less than .08 will my charges be dismissed?
- How long will this affect my record?
- What rights do I have when stopped by law enforcement?
- How is a Cannabis DUI different from an Alcohol DUI?
- How do I fight a DUI charge?
- Do I need to hire a lawyer?

After reading this book, you will be in a better position to decide if you need professional representation for your case.

As a DUI attorney in Illinois, I have represented hundreds of people who have faced DUI charges. Most people who are forced to navigate our complex system of criminal justice are scared, confused, and unsure about how to proceed with their case. This book is meant to be an introduction to the DUI laws in Illinois and what defense strategies can be used to help ensure the best possible outcome for your case.

Many times, people who are facing DUI charges believe their case is hopeless and just want to plead guilty on the first court date to get it over with as soon as possible. This is often a mistake, as there are several collateral consequences to pleading guilty to a DUI that may include a suspension or revocation of your driving privileges. There is help available in every case, regardless of prior record or circumstances of the arrest. No case is ever hopeless.

Your first step should be to read this book in its entirety. Next, you should request a confidential case assessment with an experienced DUI defense attorney in your area. Most law offices, including mine, will offer you a free initial consultation to discuss your case and what steps you should take to protect your rights and your license. Because of that, we recommend that you speak with an attorney as soon as possible after being charged. If you are in the Northern Illinois area you may call my office to schedule your free initial case evaluation by calling (779) 500-0167. We have offices in Rockford, IL and Dekalb, IL.

Everyone who is charged with DUI should meet with a lawyer before going to Court.

No lawyer can ever make you any promises or guarantees regarding the final result in a criminal case. Although this book discusses defense strategies that have assisted clients in the past achieve dismissals, not-guilty verdicts, or reductions to lesser charges, you should know that results obtained on behalf of one client do not necessarily indicate similar results can be obtained for other clients.

CHAPTER 2

DUI IN ILLINOIS

The DUI laws in Illinois are constantly changing and the Legislature is always adding new penalties for people who are suspected of Driving Under the Influence. Simply being charged with Driving Under the Influence can have a severe impact on your job, driving privileges, and educational opportunities. The laws concerning DUI are very complicated and if you are facing DUI charges, it is important that you act quickly in order to protect your rights and your driving privileges.

In Illinois, it is not illegal to have a drink and then drive a car. When charging a DUI case, the prosecution must prove that a driver had a BAC over .08 OR the driver had so much to drink that they cannot operate a vehicle with "ordinary care".

It is a common misconception to believe that a person must be "Driving" to be arrested for Driving Under the Influence. In Illinois, the laws are written to favor prosecution of impaired individuals and it is possible for a person to be convicted of DUI when they are merely in "actual physical control" of a vehicle while they are impaired by drugs or alcohol. The phrase "actual physical control" has been debated in the appellate courts many times and there is no bright line rule for what it is. However, most lawyers seem to agree that if you're in the car with the keys, then you are in actual physical control of that vehicle. In one appellate court decision, the court concluded that a person who was zipped in a sleeping bag in the back seat of his car while the keys were on the front floorboard was in "actual physical control" of his vehicle and was convicted of "Driving" Under the Influence. Furthermore, there is no requirement that your vehicle be on a public highway to be convicted of DUI. The law provides that if you are impaired and in actual physical control of your vehicle anywhere in the state, then you are Driving Under the Influence. Technically, it is possible for a person to be convicted of DUI if he is sitting in his car with the keys even while parked in his garage or driveway.

WHAT RIGHTS DO I HAVE WHEN STOPPED BY THE POLICE?

When you are stopped for DUI or any other traffic offense, you have several rights guaranteed to you by our judicial system including the right to remain silent. You are not required to answer any questions or participate in field sobriety testing. Often times, police officers will try to bolster their case against you by asking about where you are going, where you are coming from, or how much you had to drink. It is important to remember that anything you say during this encounter with the police may be used against you at a hearing or trial.

CHAPTER 3

THE PROCESS OF A DUI ARREST

THE STOP

Almost every DUI arrest involves a police officer pulling over a driver for some sort of traffic violation. These can vary from speeding, to improper lane use, to not having an updated registration sticker on your car. The important thing to remember is that a traffic stop is considered a seizure and implicates the fourth amendment. Prior to conducting a traffic stop, the constitution requires police to gather enough evidence to establish "reasonable suspicion" that the motorist is committing a crime or a traffic violation. This evidence may be the reading from a radar gun, witnessing a motorist cross over the center line, or running a vehicle's plate to find out that the registration is suspended. What reasonable suspicion is and how it relates to traffic stops is a subject that has been debated thousands of times in courts all across the country. If the courts determine that a police officer initiated a traffic stop without reasonable suspicion, all evidence from that stop can be suppressed and any resulting charges will likely be dismissed.

One of the few exceptions to the reasonable suspicion requirement are DUI checkpoints. A DUI checkpoint is a very robust operation whereby several police officers are stopping the flow of traffic at a certain point, usually with the assistance of orange cones and portable traffic control devices. These are usually set up during the early morning hours or during holiday weekends such as New Year's Eve, when impaired driving is more common. A driver going through the checkpoint is usually asked to present his driver's license and insurance information, and the police officer may ask a few questions to determine if further investigation is needed. While you do have to comply with the officer's request to hand over your license and insurance information, you are not required to answer any of the officer's questions about where you're going or how much you had to drink.

Even though DUI checkpoints are not subject to the reasonable suspicion requirement to stop a motorist, they are subject to other standards that must be adhered to in order to make the stop and resulting arrest valid. For instance, prior to conducting a DUI checkpoint, the police must publish information about the checkpoint, such as time, location, and purpose of the checkpoint.

Once a police officer makes contact with a driver, that officer may attempt to conduct a DUI investigation. A DUI investigation usually begins with a series of questions where the police officer tries to get the driver to admit to consumption of alcohol or that the driver was recently at a venue where alcohol is served. These questions usually include, "Where are you coming from", "Where are you going", and "How much have you had to drink tonight". The officer is also trained to look for other indicators of impairment, such as slurred speech, bloodshot glassy eyes, odor of alcohol, and a driver's dexterity when handing over requested documents such as a driver's license or an insurance card. Using a totality of the circumstances based on all the information the officer has when making contact with a driver, the officer may ask the driver to step out of the car and perform a series of standardized field sobriety tests. Again, the 4th amendment to the US constitution is implicated here and the officer may ask a driver to perform these tests only if he has enough evidence to establish "reasonable suspicion" that the driver is impaired by alcohol.

FIELD SOBRIETY TESTS

If an officer believes he has enough evidence to establish a "reasonable suspicion" that a driver is under the influence, he may elect to perform field sobriety testing to determine if the driver is impaired. Field sobriety testing has been studied and developed over many years and this has led to the standardization of those tests. The three tests that are recognized by the National Highway Traffic Safety Administration are:

- Horizontal Gaze Nystagmus Test
- Walk and Turn Test
- One Leg Stand Test

These field sobriety tests need to be administered in a certain manner in order for their results to be considered accurate by the courts. If a police officer does not administer the test pursuant to the guidelines set forth by the National Highway Traffic Safety Administration (NHTSA), then it is possible to have the results challenged at a hearing or trial.

The purpose of field sobriety testing is to give the police additional evidence against a driver during a DUI prosecution.

These tests are not easy to perform and involve standing in awkward positions for a long period of time. The scoring criterion for these tests is not disclosed to the participant at the time the tests are administered, and they are often times conducted in less than favorable conditions, usually by the side of the road with poor lighting conditions where the traffic stop has occurred.

While it used to be the motorist's absolute right to refuse field sobriety tests, there have been changes in the law that coincide with Illinois' legalization of cannabis that have attached penalties for drivers suspected of being under the influence of cannabis to require them to perform these tests or have their license suspended. This is likely due to the lack of available roadside testing devices that can assess a motorist's THC levels. It is important to note that with a DUI alcohol investigation, a motorist has an absolute right to refuse field sobriety testing without having their license suspended. It is only when an officer has *"an independent, cannabis-related factual basis giving reasonable suspicion that the person is driving or in actual physical control of a motor vehicle while impaired by the use of cannabis"* that their license may be suspended for failing to comply with these tests.

PORTABLE BREATHALYZER TEST

After the completion of Field Sobriety testing, the officer MAY OFFER a portable breathalyzer test (PBT). This breathalyzer is a portable unit that most police officers will carry around in their car. Often times police will be very forceful with drivers in trying to get them to take a PBT. It is important to note that under no circumstances are you ever required to submit to a PBT. In fact, there is case law that says it is the driver's choice on whether to take the test or not, and if it is not "offered" as a choice by the officer and instead forced on the driver, then the results of the

PBT may be suppressed.

Police Officers may even tell the driver that they cannot use the PBT result in court and that taking it will not have any ill consequences. This is not true. While it is correct to say that PBT results are not admissible at trial, PBT readings are admissible in all other court proceedings. This includes any hearings for probable cause determination such as preliminary hearings and grand jury hearings. Furthermore, If Defense counsel files a motion to quash arrest or suppress evidence, the PBT result will be admitted in that hearing as well.

ARREST

An officer will arrest someone for DUI if he believes that from the totality of the evidence the driver is impaired by alcohol or some other drug. The evidence that an officer can use to establish probable cause for an arrest may come from multiple sources. The first thing officers typically look for is any indicators of impairment in a subject's driving. These usually include: weaving, crossing the center line, varying speed, disobeying traffic control devices, or just being passed out at the wheel. They will also consider the performance on field sobriety tests, the result of the portable breathalyzer test, the driver's demeanor when interacting with law enforcement, and any unusual actions such as stumbling or using a vehicle to maintain balance when making an arrest decision.

CERTIFIED BREATHALYZER TEST

After an officer arrests a person for driving under the influence, the next step will be to ask that person for a second breath sample on a certified breathalyzer test or CBT. Unlike the PBT, the police officer must do certain things before obtaining a CBT result, which includes reading the warning to motorist and observing that individual for 20 minutes to ensure there are no foreign objects or unusual actions that may affect the CBT.

- **Warning to Motorist** – Prior to administering the CBT, a police officer must read verbatim a series of warnings that will detail what happens in the event that a person refuses a CBT or what happens when a CBT yields a result greater than .08 BAC. After reading this, the officer then must ask the individual to sign the Warning to Motorist. If the person refuses to sign, then the officer must indicate such on the warning.
- **20 minute waiting period** – After reading the warning to motorist, prior to taking the CBT, the police officer is required to observe the individual for 20 minutes to ensure that he does not put anything in his mouth that might affect the test. The officer is also looking for unusual actions such as belching, vomiting, or any other action that may cause fluids to enter a person's mouth that would affect the CBT.

After the warning to motorist and the 20 minute waiting period, the officer will ask the person to submit to a CBT. The results of this test will be printed out by the machine and the officer is required to write the result in a CBT log that tracks all breath results issued by that particular machine.

DUI CHARGE AND PRETRIAL RELEASE

After the CBT results are recorded, or refusal documented, the officer will write out the DUI tickets and tickets for any companion charges. If the case is charged as a misdemeanor, or a probationable felony, then the person will be released. If the case is enhanceable to a non-probationable felony, then the person will be taken into custody and remain there until they can be brought before a judge for a detainment hearing. If the State is able to prove by clear and convincing evidence that the defendant committed the crime, is a danger to a specific person or the community in general, and there are no set of conditions that can mitigate that danger, then the defendant will be held in custody until the case is resolved. If the state cannot meet its burden of proof, or if they do not file a petition to detain, then the defendant will be released with conditions.

LICENSE SUSPENSION AND VEHICLE IMPOUND

If the driver's test results show a BAC of .08 or more, a THC of either 5 nanograms or more per milliliter of whole blood or 10 nanograms or more per milliliter of other bodily substance, or any trace amounts of illegal drugs such as heroin or cocaine, or trace amounts of prescription drugs for which the driver is not legally prescribed, the driver will be issued a law enforcement sworn report notifying him of an upcoming statutory summary suspension.

If the driver's license is valid, a receipt is issued allowing the driver to drive for the next 45 days following arrest, prior to the beginning of the statutory summary suspension. The driver must carry this receipt in lieu of a driver's license during that time period.

The vehicle may be towed and impounded. The vehicle may be picked up after paying the tow costs and impound fee, and the person picking up the vehicle must show valid insurance and driver's license.

CHAPTER 4

FIELD SOBRIETY TESTS

Police Officers use field sobriety testing as one tool to try and determine whether a driver is impaired by alcohol, cannabis, or other drugs. If an individual performs poorly on these tests, the officer will use this to establish probable cause to arrest the driver for DUI, and these test results can be presented as evidence in court when the state prosecutes the case. Initially, law enforcement officers used a wide range of tests with no real standardization in administration or score to determine if a driver passed or failed the test. Without standardization, police officers were administering a wide variety of different tests, with different scoring systems, and the results of these test were often unreliable. Eventually, the National Highway Traffic Safety Administration (NHTSA) contracted the Southern California Research Institute (SCRI) in 1975 to develop a battery of field sobriety tests with a specific manner of administering and scoring the test in an attempt to standardize the process of evaluating drivers for impairment. As a result of this research, a battery of three tests were developed. According to the NHTSA manual for

DWI Detection and Standardized Field Sobriety Testing (which is used to train officers nationwide) when these tests are administered properly, correct decisions to arrest are made 95% of the time. Since these tests were created and their administration standardized and defined by NHTSA, almost all police departments nationwide have adopted this three-test battery when evaluating a driver for alcohol impairment. The three test battery includes the Horizontal Gaze Nystagmus Test (HGN), the Walk and Turn Test, and the One Leg Stand Test.

HORIZONTAL GAZE NYSTAGMUS TEST (HGN)

The HGN test is very recognizable from TV shows and movies. This is the test where the police officer will have the subject stand in front of him and follow his finger from side to side. The subject is instructed to keep his head forward and follow the officer's finger with his eyes only. What the police officer is looking for when conducting this test is an involuntary jerking of the eye, better known as nystagmus.

There are many different types of nystagmus but the only one that is indicative of alcohol consumption is Horizontal Gaze Nystagmus. The test parameters set forth by NHTSA are designed so the officer will only observe horizontal gaze nystagmus when administering the test. However, if the test is administered improperly, it is possible that the officer may notice other forms of nystagmus that are not indicative of alcohol consumption (such as Optokinetic Nystagmus) and mistakenly report it as Horizontal Gaze Nystagmus. This is why adherence to the NHTSA standards is essential when administering these tests, and any deviation can compromise the validity of the results.

When administering the test, the officer is required to evaluate the subject to see if there are any abnormalities with the subject's eyes. This is done by checking for resting nystagmus, equal tracking, and equal pupil size.

- Resting Nystagmus is a jerking of the eye when the eyes are looking straight forward. This condition is not frequently seen, and its presence usually indicates a pathology or consumption of high amounts of Dissociative Anesthetic such as PCP.
- Differing pupil size is usually present when the subject is affected by some medical condition or injury. This may include a head injury, neurological disorder, or having a glass eye.
- Tracking ability is checked by having the subject follow a stimulus quickly from left to right. If one eye follows the stimulus and the other eye does not, then the eyes are not tracking equally. If a subject does not have equal tracking, this may be an indication of certain medical conditions or brain injuries.

After checking for any abnormalities, the officer will then begin the substantive portion of the HGN test. During this part of the test, the administering officer will be looking for indicators of impairment, also known as clues. There are 6 possible clues on the HGN test (3 for each eye) and an officer will make an arrest decision if 4 of these clues are present.

Lack of Smooth Pursuit

- When the officer is looking for this clue, he will start by placing a stimulus (usually a pen or the officer's finger) approximately 12-15 inches directly in front of the subject's face and will instruct the subject to follow the stimulus with his eyes and not move his head during the administration of the test.

- The officer will then move the stimulus in a slow controlled manner from the center of the subject's face to the right while checking the subject's left eye. Then the officer will move the stimulus from the far right to the far left, checking the subject's right eye. This process is repeated 2 times to ensure accuracy.
- The officer is required to move the stimulus in a slow and controlled manner such that it takes 2 seconds for the stimulus to travel from the center of the subject's face to the far right and then 2 seconds to go from the far right back to the center.
- While doing this, the officer is looking for the eyes to jerk slightly as they move from left to right. An analogy that is used is that if the eyes have smooth pursuit, it will be like windshield wipers moving on a wet windshield, while lack of smooth pursuit would be like windshield wipers on a dry windshield.
- If the officer notices lack of smooth pursuit in both eyes, he will record 2 clues for this part of the test.

Distinct and Sustained Nystagmus at Maximum Deviation

- Maximum deviation is when the subject's eye has gone as far to one side as possible and there should be no white visible in the corner of the subject's eye.
- In Looking for this clue, the Officer will move the stimulus to the right side of the subject's face and hold for 4 seconds while looking for nystagmus. Then the Officer will move the stimulus to the left side of the subject's face and hold for 4 seconds while looking for nystagmus. This process is repeated to ensure accuracy.

- According to the NHTSA manual, in order to record this as a clue, the officer must observe the nystagmus for 4 continuous seconds. Often times, Officers administering this test will vary from the NHTSA guidelines and only hold the stimulus for a second or two. Should an officer conduct the test in this manner, it can invalidate the results of the test and can be challenged in a court proceeding.
- If the officer notices nystagmus in maximum deviation in both eyes, he will record 2 clues for this part of the test.

Onset of Nystagmus Prior to 45 Degrees

- According to the NHTSA Manual, the closer to center that nystagmus is observed, the higher the subject's BAC. The onset of nystagmus prior to 45 degrees attempts to determine if there is horizontal gaze nystagmus prior to maximum deviation.
- During this clue, the officer will move the stimulus from center to the right at a very slow pace. It should take approximately 4 seconds to go from center to maximum deviation. Once Nystagmus is observed, the officer will hold the stimulus steady. Afterwards the officer will reset the stimulus at the center of the subject's face and move the stimulus to the left to check the subject's right eye. This process is repeated for accuracy.
- If the officer observes onset of nystagmus in both eyes, he will record 2 clues for this part of the test.

WALK AND TURN TEST

The Walk and Turn test will be the first of two divided attention tests that are part of the three-test battery. A divided attention test will divide a subject's attention between a mental and a physical task. The theory being that a person who is impaired may be able to complete a mental task or a physical task, but accomplishing both together would be difficult.

During the Walk and turn test, the officer will place the subject in an awkward and unsteady position while the test is explained. The subject will be required to stay in this awkward position (physical task) while comprehending all the officer's instructions for completing the test (mental task). During this time, the officer must explain and demonstrate the requirements of the test pursuant to the standards articulated in the NHTSA manual. After the instruction phase, the subject will be asked to perform the test.

The test requires the subject to complete 9 heel-to-toe steps down a line, execute a turn, and return 9 heel-to-toe steps back. While performing this test, the officer will look for 8 different clues which include:

- Starts too soon
- Breaking the starting position
- Raising arms more than six inches
- Stepping off the line
- Not touching heel to toe
- Not executing a proper turn
- Stopping during the test
- Taking the wrong number of steps

An arrest decision will be made if the officer observes 2 clues. Often, officers will incorrectly document multiple clues for the same violation. For instance, a subject does not touch heel to toe on 3 different occasions, this should only be considered one clue.

ONE LEG STAND TEST

The second of the divided attention tests requires the subject to stand on one leg with the other foot raised six inches off the ground for 30 seconds while keeping his hands down by his sides. The subject will also be instructed to look at their raised foot, count out loud 1001, 1002, 1003, and so on until being told to stop. Should the subject put his foot down, he will be instructed to raise it back up again and continue the test. The officer will time the test and tell the subject to stop after 30 seconds. During this test, the officer will look for 4 different clues including:

- putting foot down
- raising arms more than six inches from the side
- swaying
- hopping to maintain balance

An arrest decision is made if the officer observes 2 clues. Again, sometimes officers will incorrectly document multiple observations of the same clue as multiple clues. For instance, if a subject puts his foot down 3 times, this should only count as one clue.

With each of the field sobriety tests, the officer MUST administer them consistent with the regulations promulgated within the NHTSA manual. Should the officer record erroneous clues or not administer the test properly, the results of the test may be challenged in court.

NON-STANDARDIZED FIELD SOBRIETY TESTS

Sometimes a police officer will not be able to conduct the standardized field sobriety tests based on the location of the stop. These are often utilized by the conservation police who stop boaters and do not have a flat dry surface available that is required by the NHTSA manual in conducting the tests. These often include the alphabet test, counting test, and touching finger to nose. Since these tests are not certified by NHTSA, their admissibility may be challenged in court.

During the alphabet test, an officer will pick 2 letters in the middle of the alphabet and ask the subject to recite the alphabet, without singing it, from one letter to the next. For instance, the officer may ask the subject to recite the alphabet from G to Q. They usually select a stopping point that begins a series of letters that are usually sung together, such as Q, because when the majority of people recite the alphabet they will say Q, R, S together. The concept behind this test is that if someone is impaired, they will forget which letter they were supposed to end on and sing their way past it.

The number test is similar to the alphabet test in that the subject will be given 2 numbers, usually about 20 numbers apart and be asked to count backwards from the first number to the last. An example would be to count backwards from 67 to 49. Again, the concept being that if someone is impaired, they will forget which number to stop on while they are counting and continue to count down past the ending number.

DRUG RELATED SOBRIETY TESTS

Certain officers receive training on additional test that have not been evaluated by NHTSA but are frequently used when a person may be under the influence of drugs. The two main tests that are used are the Modified Romberg Test and the Lack of Convergence Test.

During the Modified Romberg Test, the subject is instructed to stand with their feet together, arms at their sides, their head tilted backwards, and eyes closed. The subject will then be asked to estimate the passage of 30 seconds. Once 30 seconds has elapsed, they are instructed to look forward and open their eyes. When the officer tells the subject to begin, he will start timing. During this test, the officer is looking for 3 different indicators: swaying, eye or body tremors, and time estimation. The theory being, a person who is under the influence of cannabis, heroine, or other downer drugs, would take substantially longer to estimate the passage of 30 seconds. While a person who is under the influence of cocaine, methamphetamines, or any other upper drugs, would estimate the passage of 30 seconds very quickly.

The lack of convergence test involves the officer telling the subject to follow a stimulus while he moves it in a circle around the subject's head. Then the officer will continue to move the stimulus in smaller circles until the stimulus settles about 2 inches from the bridge of the subject's nose, requiring the subject to cross his eyes to stay focused on the stimulus. Should the subject be unable to cross his eyes, this would be considered a sign of impairment and an indicator that he is under the influence of drugs.

CHAPTER 5

WHAT WILL HAPPEN TO MY LICENSE FOLLOWING A DUI ARREST?

In Illinois, it is possible for your license to be suspended, even if you are found not guilty of Driving Under the Influence. This is because Illinois is an "implied consent" state. Basically, this means that by driving on a public highway in Illinois, you have automatically given consent for any law enforcement officer to perform chemical testing to determine your BAC. The officer only needs a minimal amount of evidence to believe that you are driving impaired prior to asking for chemical testing. If you refuse the officer's request, then your license will be automatically suspended, and this suspension will not be dependent on the outcome of the underlying DUI case.

STATUTORY SUMMARY SUSPENSION

A statutory summary suspension provides for the automatic suspension of driving privileges of a driver who fails or refuses chemical testing pursuant to the implied consent laws. Failure of chemical testing means a driver has a BAC of .08 or more, a THC concentration of either 5 nanograms or more per milliliter of whole blood or 10 nanograms or more per milliliter of any other bodily substance, or trace amounts of illegal drugs such as heroin or cocaine, or trace amounts of prescription drugs for which the driver does not have a prescription. This suspension will become effective on the 46th day from the date of the suspension notice.

FIELD SOBRIETY TEST SUSPENSION

With the recent legalization of recreational marijuana in Illinois, the Legislature has decided to up the penalties for those who are suspected of driving under the influence of cannabis. A Field Sobriety Test Suspension is only applicable for DUI cannabis cases, and it allows for the suspension of driving privileges should a driver, suspected of being under the influence of cannabis, refuse to participate in field sobriety testing, or fail field sobriety testing. Prior to issuing the suspension, however, the police officer must read the driver a warning to motorist detailing what will happen should he refuse or fail testing.

One very important distinction between a field sobriety test suspension and a statutory summary suspension is that the driver will not be eligible to receive a Monitoring Device Driving Permit (MDDP) that would allow driving privileges during the period of suspension. Whereas a person who has their license suspended under the statutory summary suspension would possibly be eligible for a MDDP that will allow them to drive during the period of suspension, provided they operated a vehicle equipped with a Breath Alcohol Interlock Ignition Device (BAIID).

CHALLENGING THE STATUTORY SUMMARY SUSPENSION

You do have a right to challenge this suspension and in order to do so, you must file a petition with the circuit court within 90 days from the date that your notice of suspension was issued (usually the date of your arrest). Whenever you file this petition, this will begin a civil proceeding whereby you are challenging the State on its basis to suspend your license. Just because you file a petition to challenge your suspension, this does not stop the suspension from taking effect.

Since challenging this suspension is a civil matter and not criminal, the rules of evidence, burden of proof, and standard of proof are all different than in the underlying DUI case. The most important distinction is that, as the petitioner, YOU have the burden of proof and not the State's Attorney's Office to show that they were in the wrong for suspending your license. Furthermore, the standard of proof is not beyond a reasonable doubt, as it is in criminal cases. Instead, you must show by a preponderance of the evidence (more likely than not) that the State did not have a basis to suspend your license.

When you file a petition to challenge the suspension of your license there are technically only 5 statutorily defined defenses that you may allege in order to reverse the suspension of your license. These defenses must be listed in the petition or you waive your right to have them heard. The 5 statutory bases for a rescission are as follows:

- The Defendant was not properly put under arrest for an offense as defined under section 11-501 of the Illinois Vehicle Driving Code or similar provision of a local ordinance, as evidenced by the issuance of a Uniform Traffic Ticket or other form of charge.

- The arresting officer did not have reasonable grounds to believe that the Defendant was driving or in actual physical control of a motor vehicle while under the influence of alcohol or drugs, or a combination thereof.
- The Defendant was not properly warned by the arresting officer as provided in Section 11-501.1 of the Illinois Vehicle Code, upon the request of the arresting officer.
- The Defendant did not refuse to submit and/or complete the required chemical tests, pursuant to Section 11-501.1 of the Illinois Vehicle Code, upon the request of the arresting officer.
- The Defendant submitted to the requested test but the test sample of the Defendant's blood alcohol concentration did not indicate a BAC of .08 or more.

In addition to the statutory defenses, you may also claim that you were not operating a vehicle on a public roadway or that the arresting officer submitted a defective sworn report. A sworn report will be considered defective if the Secretary of State is unable to confirm the start date or the length of the suspension. This usually happens when the officer failed to check one of the boxes on the form or put the wrong date for when the notice was issued.

Once you file a petition to challenge the Statutory Summary Suspension (SSS), the State has 30 days to give you a hearing on your petition. If for any reason they cannot hear your petition within that time period, your suspension will be rescinded. There are 2 main reasons that the State would not be able to give you a hearing within this time period: The Secretary of State has not confirmed the suspension of your license or the State has not tendered all the discovery you need to present a prima facie case on your petition.

If the Secretary of State has not confirmed the suspension within 30 days of filing your petition, there is case law that says you get an automatic rescission. It should be noted that there is a district split for this case law, meaning not all districts will allow this. If you are in Cook County, then this will not be a basis to rescind the suspension. However, there are cases from the second and third district, that every other county in Illinois seems to follow, that will allow for a rescission should the Secretary of State not confirm the suspension. A suspension is usually not confirmed if the arresting officer fails to send in the sworn report to the Secretary of State, which frequently happens when there is a blood draw and there is a delay between the DUI arrest and the issuance of a sworn report, or the arresting officer fails to fill out the form properly.

There is also case law that says if the State does not give you all the discovery you need to present a prima facie case, then you are entitled to a rescission. In order to get a rescission on this basis, you must file a timely motion for discovery, accompanied with your petition, and meet with the State's Attorney to discuss outstanding discovery issues. Also, the missing discovery must be directly relevant to the rescission of the suspension. For instance, if the State fails to provide you with portable breathalyzer test certification logs, it may still proceed forward with the hearing, but it will not be able to use the breathalyzer result as evidence during the hearing. However, if they fail to provide Certified Breathalyzer Test logs, squad/body camera videos, police reports, or booking videos, then this can be fatal to their case and a rescission should be ordered.

HOW LONG WILL MY LICENSE BE SUSPENDED?

The length of suspension is based on a couple of factors. First, did you refuse chemical testing or fail chemical testing? Second, have you had a DUI or DUI license suspension within the last 5 years? If you have not had a DUI within the last 5 years, you will be considered a "first offender" for purposes of determining the length of the license suspension and whether you are eligible for a driving permit during that period of suspension. It's important to note that for the criminal case, previous DUI convictions will never drop off your record and even though you are considered a first offender for the purposes of license suspension, this will not be reflected in the criminal case if you have a DUI conviction that is more than 5 years old.

Failing Chemical Testing

- First offense — Suspension of driving privileges for six months (eligible for a Monitoring Device Driving Permit)
- Second or subsequent offense within five years — Suspension of driving privileges for one year. (No MDDP eligibility but may apply for an RDP)

Refusing to Submit to Chemical Testing

- First offense — Suspension of driving privileges for 12 months (eligible for a Monitoring Device Driving Permit)
- Second or subsequent offense within five years — Suspension of driving privileges for three years. (No MDDP eligibility but may apply for an RDP)

FIELD SOBRIETY TEST SUSPENSION

If a law enforcement officer has reasonable suspicion to believe you are driving or in actual physical control of a motor vehicle while impaired by the use of cannabis, they may ask you to submit to standardized field sobriety tests. If you refuse or fail to complete standardized field sobriety tests or if the tests disclose you are impaired by the use of cannabis, a field sobriety test suspension will be imposed. **A Field Sobriety Test Suspension only applies to DUI Cannabis cases.**

Your driver's license may be suspended for both a field sobriety test suspension and a statutory summary suspension at the same time.

Suspension length for Field Sobriety Test Suspension

- **Refusing Field Sobriety Testing** – Suspension of driving privileges for 12 months (not eligible for an MDDP).
- **Failing Field Sobriety Testing** – Suspension of driving privileges for six months (not eligible for an MDDP).

DRIVERS UNDER 21 – ZERO TOLERANCE SUSPENSION

If a driver under age 21 is convicted of DUI, he or she will face the revocation of their driving privileges for a minimum of two years for a first conviction. If a driver under age 21, is stopped and issued a citation for a traffic violation and is found to have any trace of alcohol in their system or they refuse chemical testing while operating a motor vehicle, his or her driving privileges will be suspended. It is at the discretion of the investigating officer and based on test results or a test refusal whether a traffic stop results in a Zero Tolerance Suspension or Statutory Summary Suspension.

If a driver's license was suspended prior to age 21, the driver will be required to successfully complete a driver remedial education course to make their driving privileges valid again. In addition, they may be required to submit to a complete driver's license examination to be re-issued a driver's license.

Zero Tolerance Failed Chemical Testing

- **First offense** — 3-month suspension of driving privileges for a BAC of more than .00.
- **Second offense** — 1-year suspension of driving privileges for a BAC of more than .00.

Zero Tolerance Refused Chemical Testing

- **First violation** — 6-month suspension of driving privileges for refusal or failure to complete a BAC test.
- **Second violation** — 2-year suspension of driving privileges for refusal or failure to complete a BAC test.

Note: Full driving privileges may not be restored until all applicable reinstatement fees are paid to the Secretary of State's office.

Under 21 DUI Penalties

Any person under age 21 also may be charged with a DUI: if he/she has a BAC of .08 or more; more than .05 with additional evidence proving impairment; any illegal drugs in his/her system; or other indications of impaired driving.

- First DUI conviction — Minimum 2-year revocation of driving privileges.
- Second DUI conviction — Minimum 5-year revocation of driving privileges.

CAN I GET A DRIVING PERMIT?

If you are considered a first offender for purposes of the Statutory Summary Suspension, then you will be eligible for a Monitoring Device Driving Permit (MDDP). This is a permit that will let you drive anytime and anywhere, as long as you operate a vehicle that is equipped with a Breath Alcohol Ignition Interlock Device (BAIID). There can be exceptions made to the BAIID requirement if you are driving a work vehicle for work purposes. To obtain this exception, you must provide information to the Illinois Secretary of State about your employment and vehicles when applying for the MDDP.

The application for the MDDP will be mailed to you once the suspension on your license is confirmed by the Secretary of State. Along with this application, you will receive information about when your suspension will go into effect and how long this suspension will last. Furthermore, there will be Information about how to pay the reinstatement fee on your license once the suspension has termed. It is advisable to pay the reinstatement fee at least one month prior to your license suspension ending. If you fail to pay the fee and your MDDP expires, you will not have valid driving privileges and could be arrested for driving with a suspended license. To check the status of your license, you may use the Secretary of State's automated system by calling **(217) 785-8619**. You can also download a copy of the MDDP application from the secretary of State's website at https://www.ilsos.gov/publications/pdf_publications/baiid24.pdf

One important note is mail from the Secretary of State is not forwardable, meaning, if you have recently moved and have sent a forwarding address to the post office, mail from the Secretary of State will be returned instead of being forwarded to your new

address. The Secretary of State requires you to notify them of an address change within 10 days from the time that you move. You can notify them by going to a Driver Services facility or you can download a form from their website and mail it in. The change of address form is located at
https://www.ilsos.gov/publications/pdf_publications/vsd165.pdf

You will have a grace period of 45 days between the time you are charged with DUI until the suspension goes into effect. Since, it can take up to 30 days to process the MDDP application, it is important that you get it in the mail as soon as you receive it to ensure that there is no down time with your driving privileges.

RESTRICTED DRIVING PERMIT

If your license is suspended and you have a prior DUI or DUI based licensed suspension within the last 5 years, then you will not be eligible for an MDDP. In these cases, the only driving relief you will be eligible for is a Restricted Driving Permit (RDP). An RDP would give you driving privileges for specific purposes and specific times, such as going to work or doctor's visits. This is very difficult to obtain and you must have a hearing with the Secretary of State in order to get this type of permit. The process of applying for and receiving an RDP usually takes about 6 months and it is not guaranteed. The first step in getting an RDP is to apply for a formal hearing with the Secretary of State, and it is usually 2 months between the application and the actual hearing. After the hearing you usually have to wait 2-3 months before you receive a decision from the Secretary of State notifying you whether you have been approved or not. These hearings are not trivial, and many people are denied on their first attempt, meaning they would have to go through the entire process of re-applying before they receive the permit. A lot of times, if the suspension is only one year, there would not be a lot of benefit in going through this process.

LICENSE REVOCATION

In addition to any suspension that you may incur for failing or refusing chemical testing, your license may also become revoked if you get a conviction for the DUI criminal case. A revocation has severe consequences for your driving privileges and acts as an indefinite suspension. To remove a driving revocation from your license, you will be required to have a hearing with the Secretary of State before you can regain any driving privileges. This can be a very onerous process and essentially you are required to present evidence to the hearing officer that you are not in danger of reoffending.

Usually license revocations occur after someone is found guilty of a DUI. However, there are mechanisms to revoke driving privileges without a finding of guilt. This is done when there is a DUI that involves great bodily harm or death. An administrative driver's license revocation is handled by the Secretary of State and requires cooperation with the county State's Attorney's Office. Drivers who are charged with DUI or another serious offense may have their driving privileges revoked without a hearing only after the Secretary of State receives sufficient evidence from a State's Attorney's Office that there was an accident involving great bodily harm or death. This is referred to as a Statutory Summary Revocation, and you are not allowed to challenge this revocation in court. Instead, you must have an administrative hearing with the Secretary of State to challenge the revocation. In the event of a revocation, driving privileges remain revoked until the case is adjudicated, and often times this revocation can last for years. Additionally, reinstatement of driving privileges is not guaranteed and the reinstatement process is often expensive and time consuming.

CHAPTER 6

WHAT WILL HAPPEN TO MY CDL IF I GET A DUI?

A DUI can have serious consequences for persons with a commercial driver's license. For ordinary drivers, dispositions like Court Supervision are available to keep DUI convictions off their record and prevent their license from becoming revoked. While a CDL holder may receive Court Supervision for their DUI, this will not prevent their CDL from being disqualified. For a first offense DUI, a CDL holder will have their commercial driver's license disqualified for a period one year. If the driver was hauling hazardous materials, then the disqualification would be for 3 years. A second violation, regardless of the circumstances, will result in a lifetime disqualification.

A CDL driver does not have to be convicted of a DUI to be disqualified from operating Commercial Motor Vehicles (CMV). Since Illinois is an "implied consent" state, any driver on the public roadway is required to submit to a breathalyzer when asked. If the driver refuses chemical testing, their license will be subject to a Statutory Summary Suspension (SSS). In addition to the SSS, a CDL holder will have their license disqualified for any of the following:

- The driver refuses to submit to a breathalyzer
- The driver has a BAC over .08 while operating their personal vehicle
- The driver has a BAC over .04 while operating a CMV

It is possible for a CDL driver to be found not guilty of a DUI and still have their CDL disqualified. In order to prevent the disqualification of a CDL you must avoid a conviction to the DUI charge AND get the Statutory Summary Suspension removed from your license. There are several ways to avoid a DUI conviction that include:

- Getting the Charge amended or reduced to a reckless driving or some other offense that does not involve a mandatory CDL disqualification
- Argue a motion to quash the arrest and suppress evidence based on lack of probable cause to arrest for DUI or effectuate a traffic stop
- Get the prosecutor to voluntarily dismiss the case
- Get acquitted at trial

In addition to avoiding a DUI conviction, you will also have to remove the Statutory Summary Suspension from your license in order to preserve your CDL. In order to do this, you must file a petition to rescind statutory summary suspension within 90 days of being served notice of suspension. If you do not file a timely petition, you will lose your right to challenge the suspension. Once the petition is filed, it will have to be granted by the court, which can be accomplished through any of the following:

- Have the prosecutor agree to rescind the suspension as part of a plea OR
- Have a hearing on the petition and prove by a preponderance of evidence (more likely than not) any of the following
  - The arresting officer did not have a valid basis to initiate a traffic stop
  - The arresting officer did not have probable cause to arrest for DUI
  - That you submitted to chemical testing that did not show you were over the limit
  - That you did not refuse to submit to chemical testing
  - That you were not read the warning to motorist prior to chemical testing (or the warning to motorist was not signed)
  - That the police submitted a defective notice of summary suspension to the Secretary of State
  - That you were on private property

It is very difficult to avoid a DUI charge and remove the Statutory Summary Suspension from your license, however, this is not impossible. An experienced DUI attorney will be able to build a solid defense to fight the case and possibly negotiate a deal with the prosecution that will prevent your CDL from being disqualified.

CHAPTER 7

WILL A DUI CONVICTION GO ON MY RECORD?

In Illinois, a DUI conviction is considered both a criminal offense and a traffic offense. Because of this, if you are convicted, the DUI will go on both your criminal record as well as your driving record.

There are currently no mechanisms in Illinois to provide for an expungement or removal of a DUI conviction from a criminal record. If you are convicted, you should expect that record will remain for the rest of your life. This is a very serious consequence, and will affect you in many ways including:

- Employment Applications
- Background Checks
- Security Clearances
- Professional Licensing

In Illinois, arrest records are public information. As soon as you are taken to jail, a public record is created so that anyone searching these records will discover this arrest. This means that if you have to undergo a background check, your pending case is likely to show up. It will not show you as being convicted or guilty of DUI, just that you were arrested.

COURT SUPERVISION

Court Supervision is a great way to avoid a conviction on a first offense DUI. If you receive court supervision for your DUI, the court will continue the case for a period of up to 2 years. As long as you complete all the conditions of your sentence and do not violate the law within that time, the case will be dismissed at the end of the supervision period. The usual conditions of DUI court supervision include, completing alcohol treatment as recommended by a DUI evaluation (between 10 and 75 hours), attending a DUI victim impact panel, paying a fine, and possibly performing community service hours.

If you have a professional license, you may be required to report all convictions to your licensing board. Getting court supervision will help avoid a conviction and may help you keep your professional license. Some professional licenses only require you to report convictions for criminal offenses. Since court supervision is not technically a conviction, you may not have to report this to the licensing board. You should always consult the rules of your licensing board to confirm their reporting requirements.

While court supervision is not a conviction on your record and will avoid a license revocation for in-state residence, this may not be the case for out of state drivers. Most states do not recognize Illinois' court supervision and if you have an out of state license, the foreign state will likely count this as a conviction. This is important, because most other state's will suspend or revoke a person's driving privileges if they are convicted of DUI. If you get a DUI in Illinois and have an out of state license, you should always consult with an attorney in your home state prior to resolving your DUI case in Illinois, as there may be several collateral consequences to a plea that an attorney in Illinois would not be aware of.

EXPUNGEMENT

While most criminal cases in Illinois that are resolved with court supervision are eligible to be expunged or sealed, this does not apply to DUI. The only way to get a DUI case expunged off your record is if the State's Attorney dismisses the case, or you are found not guilty at trial. While a DUI conviction can be avoided with court supervision, the arrest record cannot be expunged.

CHAPTER 8

WHAT ARE THE PENALTIES FOR DRIVING UNDER THE INFLUENCE?

In addition to the license suspension and revocation, the Driving Under the Influence charge can have severe criminal penalties that can involve potential jail time or even time in the Department of Corrections depending on the severity of the charge and a person's previous record.

FIRST OFFENSE DUI

For a first time DUI charge, this will usually be charged as a Class A misdemeanor which has a range of penalties including up to one year in jail and fines of up to $2,500 (plus additional mandatory fees). Court Supervision is a possibility for a first offense DUI, assuming there are no other aggravating factors. Court Supervision is a great way to keep a conviction off your record and avoid a driver's license revocation. Essentially, when you receive court supervision, the court will continue the case for a period of time (usually between 12 and 24 months) and, if you complete all the requirements of the order and do not pick up any more charges during that period, the case will be dismissed. Usual requirements for a DUI court supervision order include completing alcohol treatment, attending a one-time DUI Victim Impact Panel, and not consuming any alcohol during that period. While court supervision is a great disposition for a first offense DUI, it is not guaranteed and a conviction is still possible. If you are convicted of DUI, even on your first offense, your driving privileges will be revoked.

Possible Penalties for First Offense DUI

- If a conviction enters, a minimum revocation of driving privileges for one year (two years if driver is under age 21); suspension of vehicle registration
- If committed with a BAC of .16 or more there is an additional mandatory minimum fine of $500 and mandatory minimum 100 hours of community service
- If committed while transporting a child under age 16 — In addition to any penalties or fines, possible imprisonment of up to six months, mandatory minimum fine of $1,000 and 25 days of community service in a program benefiting children
- If committed while driver's license was suspended or revoked, or while operating an uninsured vehicle, the case can be enhanced to a class 4 felony and has the potential for 1 to 3 years in the department of corrections

SECOND OFFENSE DUI

A second offense DUI will usually be charged as a class A misdemeanor, assuming there are no other aggravating factors. Unfortunately, court supervision will not be an available disposition for a second or subsequent DUI. Additionally, there is a mandatory minimum sentence of 5 days in jail or 240 hours of public service work that will be required upon a conviction. A conviction for a second offense DUI will lead to a revocation of driving privileges in addition to any suspension that might have occurred for failing or refusing chemical testing. This license revocation would invalidate any driving permit including a Monitoring Device Driving Permit (MDDP) which may be available to drivers during their statutory summary suspension.

Handling a second offense DUI is drastically different than a first offense because any disposition will lead to a revocation of driving privileges. In order to avoid the license revocation and potentially a substantial period of time without driving privileges, one of the following must occur:

- The DUI charge will have to be reduced or amended to something other than Driving Under the Influence, usually Reckless Driving
- The DUI charge is outright dismissed
- The case is litigated at trial and a not guilty verdict is returned

There are several strategies and techniques that can be employed to give someone the best chance of avoiding a license revocation when facing a second offense DUI. These include getting treatment done prior to disposition, undergoing SCRAM monitoring, and presenting mitigation to the State's Attorney.

Possible Penalties for Second Offense DUI

- A minimum revocation of driving privileges for one year, suspension of vehicle registration. If this is a second conviction (i.e. did not receive court supervision on the first offense), the minimum revocation will be extended to 5 years.
- Mandatory minimum 5 days in jail or 240 hours of public service work.
- If committed with a BAC of .16 or more there is an additional mandatory minimum fine of $1,250 and an additional 2 days in jail above all other mandatory minimum sentences.
- If committed while transporting a child under age 16, the case can be enhanced to a class 2 felony which has a potential for 3 to 7 years in the Department of Corrections. In addition to any penalties or fines, possible imprisonment of up to six months, mandatory minimum fine of $5,000 and 25 days of community service in a program benefiting children.
- If committed while driver's license was suspended or revoked, or while operating an uninsured vehicle, the case can be enhanced to a class 4 felony and has the potential for 1 to 3 years in the department of corrections.

FELONY DUI

In Illinois, there are several ways that a DUI can become a felony. Even if it is your first offense for Driving Under the Influence, your case can still be enhanced to a felony under certain circumstances. The approach to representing a client charged with a felony DUI is drastically different than representing a client with a misdemeanor DUI charge. It is imperative that a fully comprehensive defense strategy be designed and implemented as soon as possible after an arrest in order to provide for the best possible outcome.

CLASS 4 FELONY AGGRAVATED DUI

While a misdemeanor DUI charge has a sentence of no more than one year in jail, a Class 4 Felony Aggravated DUI has a sentencing range of 1-3 years in prison. While the proof is the same as a misdemeanor DUI, a felony DUI will have one or more additional facts that trigger the more serious sentencing range. All Class 4 felony DUIs are first or second offense DUIs with an additional factor that includes:

- Not having a valid Driver's license
- Not having insurance
- Driving with a suspended license
- Being involved in an accident resulting in Great Bodily Harm

If a person is convicted of a Class 4 Felony DUI, the minimum sentence that can be given by the court is a term of probation or conditional discharge with 10 days in jail or 480 hours of public service work. There are circumstances where a class 4 DUI can have extended sentencing ranges. For instance if a person commits a DUI that results in great bodily harm to another person, the sentencing range is 1-12 years in prison, however the person is still eligible for probation.

THIRD OFFENSE DUI

A third offense DUI will be charged as a class 2 felony, with a sentencing range of 3-7 years in prison. Even if you received court supervision on your first DUI and the case was eventually dismissed, this still counts as an "offense" in the eyes of the law.

Therefore, if a person receives supervision on their first DUI and a conviction on their second, the court will still consider this as two prior offenses. A third offense DUI is a "probationable" class 2 felony. This means that if a person is convicted, the court may sentence them to serve a term of probation in lieu of the mandatory 3-7 years in prison. If the court does sentence a person to probation, the minimum sentence is 10 days in jail or 480 hours of public service work. If at the time of the offense, a person has a BAC > .16 then the minimum sentence is increased 90 days in jail. There are also other circumstances where a third offense may involve an extended sentencing range, such as being involved in an accident that resulted in the death of another.

Minimum Sentence for Third Offense DUI

- Probationable Class 2 felony
- Mandatory minimum 10 days in jail or 480 hours of public service work
- If BAC > .16 mandatory minimum 90 days in jail

FOURTH, FIFTH AND SIXTH OFFENSE DUI

The court is not allowed to give probation to any person convicted of a fourth or subsequent offense for Driving Under the Influence. A fourth offense DUI is a "non-probationable" class 2 felony. This means that if a person is convicted, the court must sentence them to 3-7 years in prison. If the case is extended term eligible, then the sentencing range is 3-14 years in prison. In addition to the term in prison, any person convicted of a fourth or subsequent DUI that had a BAC > .16 will be subject to a mandatory minimum fine of $5,000. If they were transporting a person under the age 16 at the time, the mandatory minimum fine is increased to $25,000.

Penalties for Fourth, Fifth, and Sixth DUI

- Fourth Offense - Class 2 Felony 3-7 years in prison
- Fifth Offense – Class 1 Felony 4-15 years in prison
- Sixth and Subsequent Offense – Class X Felony 6-30 years in prison
- If BAC > .16 mandatory minimum fine of $5,000
- If transporting a person under the age of 16, mandatory minimum fine of $25,000

AGGRAVATED DUI WITH DEATH

A first offense DUI that results in the death of another person, and the violation was the proximate cause of death to that person, then it will be charged as a class 2 felony with a sentencing range of 3-14 years in prison. If the DUI resulted in the death of 2 or more people, then the sentencing range is 6-28 years in prison. Furthermore, truth in sentencing applies and any person sentenced will not receive day for day (50%) credit on their sentence. Instead, any person sentenced for a DUI involving death must serve 85% of their prison sentence. DUI Death cases are extremely complex and it's important to hire an experienced attorney to represent you.

Penalties for DUI with Death

- Class 2 felony 3-14 years in prison
- If accident results in the death or 2 or more people, sentencing range is 6-28 years in prison
- Truth in sentencing applies 85% of time must be served.

CHAPTER 9

DUI DRUG

DUI Laws in Illinois apply to people who are under the influence of alcohol as well as persons who may be under the influence of drugs. If a police officer suspects that you are under the influence of any type of drug, even prescription drugs, you may be arrested for DUI. While the elements of a DUI-Drug case are similar to that of a DUI-Alcohol case, in that the prosecution has to prove a person was impaired while in actual physical control of a vehicle, proving impairment by drugs often requires expert testimony. Because most police officers are not qualified as experts, the court will not allow them to opine as to whether a person is impaired by a particular drug. This can make it difficult for the prosecution to be able to lay the proper foundation to admit all the evidence they need to secure a conviction for a DUI drug case. An experienced defense attorney will be able to take advantage of these evidentiary requirements in order to get the best disposition possible.

OVER THE COUNTER MEDICATIONS AND PRESCRIPTION DRUGS

Even if you are taking over the counter medications, or medications for which you have a prescription, you may still be arrested for DUI Drug. Just because you are legally consuming medication does not mean the State won't bring charges against you. In a DUI-Alcohol case, the State may prove impairment based on a breath test or standardized field sobriety testing. In a DUI Drug case the state must prove BOTH that you were taking a substance that has an impairing effect AND that you were actually impaired from the consumption of that substance. Evidence of this type is only admissible through expert testimony. It is often the case that the police officer making the arrest does not have the proper training or qualifications to determine if a person is legally under the influence of drugs. An experienced attorney will take advantage of this and move to suppress any evidence obtained by an unqualified or untrained police officer.

CONTROLLED SUBSTANCES - STRICT LIABILITY

Driving while under the influence of any controlled substance for which you do not have a prescription is considered a strict liability crime. This applies to prescription medications that have an impairing effect and to illegal drugs such as cocaine or heroin. Being a strict liability offense means the State does not have to prove that you were actually impaired by the substance at the time of driving. The only thing the State must show is the driver had trace amounts of a controlled substance in their system while operating a vehicle. Depending on the substance consumed, there can be trace amounts in a person's system for several days, long after the effects of the drug have worn off. This means a person who has consumed controlled substances several days prior to driving a car is potentially guilty of DUI.

SHOULD I SUBMIT TO CHEMICAL TESTING?

Unfortunately, it is the reality of our system we live in that the people who cooperate with law enforcement usually suffer the worst consequences. If a person has consumed a controlled substance a week ago and shows no signs of impairment, the only way the State could get a conviction is if the driver were to voluntarily give a urine sample to the police. If a person shows no signs of impairment and does not submit to chemical testing, it will be nearly impossible for the State to prove their case. If you refuse testing or you submit to a test that shows trace amounts of a controlled substance in your system, then your license will be suspended.

DUI DEATH AND STRICT LIABILITY LAWS

DUI Death is a serious charge with a sentencing range of 3-14 years in prison. Until recently, the only thing the State had to prove was that a person had trace amounts of a controlled substance in their system and that person was involved in an accident that caused the death of another. The law did not consider whose fault the accident was or whether the person was actually impaired at the time of the accident.

Recent case law has changed this and the State is now charged with showing BOTH that the person was impaired by a substance AND that impairment was the proximate cause of the accident. DUI-Death cases are extremely complicated, especially when there is an issue of impairment by drugs. Expert testimony will be an integral part of an effective defense strategy that will show a break in the causal relationship between the presence of trace amounts of drugs in a person's system and a traffic accident that caused the death of another.

DUI COMBINATION DRUGS AND ALCOHOL

Additionally, if the police believe that a driver is under the combined influence of alcohol and drugs, then they may charge that person with a DUI based on the combined influence. This charge is usually present when a person has a BAC less than .08 or the person admits to the police officer that they were consuming some sort of prescription medication that has an impairing effect. The statute provides that a person is guilty of DUI if they are *"under the combined influence of alcohol, other drug or drugs, or intoxicating compound or compounds to a degree that renders the person incapable of safely driving."* This can sometimes be a difficult charge for the prosecutor to prove up. To secure a conviction, the prosecution will have to prove all of the following beyond a reasonable doubt:

- A person was driving, or in actual physical control of a vehicle
- The driver is at least partially impaired by alcohol
- The driver had consumed some type of drug
- That drug had an impairing effect
- The driver was impaired by that drug while operating their vehicle

It is often very difficult for the prosecution to get a conviction on this type of charge, because they will need expert testimony to prove that a particular type of drug has an impairing effect AND that the driver was under the influence of that particular drug at the time of driving. It is not enough for an unqualified police officer to testify that a person merely looked like he was on drugs, or that he was acting crazy so he had to be taking something.

WHAT THE STATE HAS TO PROVE

While the elements of a DUI Drug and Alcohol may be similar, the State will have a couple of extra hurdles to jump through before securing a conviction for DUI Drug cases. With most DUI-Drug cases, the arresting officer will not be qualified to opine to the court that a person was under the influence of drugs. Most police officers are not trained as drug recognition examiners (DRE) and will be barred in court from testifying about a person's impairment to drugs. Even if a police officer is qualified as a DRE, this usually will only include illegal drugs such as heroin, cocaine, etc.

When the state tries to prosecute based on impairment from prescription drugs, they will need more than the testimony of a DRE qualified police officer. There are several types of prescription medications out there and each of them have differing effects. When prosecuting a DUI-Drug case based on prescription medication, the state will have to prove the following

- The person was driving or in actual physical control of a vehicle
- The person consumed a prescription medication
- That particular medication has an impairing effect (expert testimony required)
- That the driver was impaired by that medication (expert testimony required)

When you get into the arena of prescription drugs, even police officers that are qualified as drug recognition examiners, may not have the ability to detect the effects of the different prescription medications that are out there. Additionally, when proving that a particular medication has an impairing effect, a police officer's testimony will not be sufficient. The prosecution will be required to present expert testimony from a doctor or a pharmacist that is familiar with the effects of the drug that was allegedly consumed.

CHAPTER 10

DUI CANNABIS

Until recently, the laws of Illinois involving cannabis were similar to the DUI drug laws and specified that anyone operating a vehicle with trace amounts of cannabis in their system would be guilty of a DUI. Even if a person consumed marijuana 3 days prior and the effects of the drug had long since worn off, the legislature still considered it a serious offense even though the driver was not impaired at the time. Recently the laws have changed with the legalization of cannabis in Illinois and now considers the levels of cannabis that are in a person's system. The new laws specify that it is illegal to operate a vehicle with a THC concentration of 5 nanograms or more per milliliter of whole blood or 10 nanograms or more per milliliter of other bodily substance, such as urine or saliva. If a person refuses chemical testing, the State would then be required to show that both a person had consumed cannabis and was in fact impaired by cannabis at the time of driving to sustain a conviction. Absent any statements from the driver, this can be a very difficult hill for the prosecution to climb, especially if the arresting officer does not have specialized training in drug detection.

DO I HAVE TO DO FIELD SOBRIETY TESTING?

This is a tricky question, and the answer has changed with recent changes in the law concerning cannabis DUI cases. Traditionally, a driver in Illinois had an absolute right under the 4th amendment to refuse all chemical testing and field sobriety testing. That is still true to some extent. However, the Illinois legislature has decided to up the penalties for persons who refuse or fail field sobriety testing as it relates to driving privileges of motorists suspected of being under the influence of cannabis.

Illinois is considered an implied consent state, which means, if you are on the roadways within the state, you have already given consent to submit to chemical testing. If you choose not to cooperate, the secretary of state will suspend your license, regardless of whether you are eventually found not guilty of the underlying DUI charge. The implied consent statute is listed below.

> 625 ILCS 5/11-501.1
>
> *(a) Any person who drives or is in actual physical control of a motor vehicle upon the public highways of this State shall be deemed to have given consent … to a chemical test or tests of blood, breath, other bodily substance, or urine for the purpose of determining the content of alcohol, other drug or drugs, or intoxicating compound or compounds*

While refusing chemical testing can lead to a license suspension, it has always been the right of motorists within the state to refuse field sobriety testing. Under the new law, drivers who are suspected of being under the influence of cannabis will have their license suspended for one year (three years for repeat offenders) if they refuse field sobriety testing and six months (one year for repeat offenders) if they fail. The new law allows for a license suspension when:

1. The officer has reasonable suspicion that the motorist was in actual physical control of a vehicle while impaired by cannabis (mere possession of a medical cannabis card is not a sufficient basis for reasonable suspicion) AND
2. The officer warns the motorist that refusal to participate to field sobriety testing will result in a suspension of driving privileges AND
3. The motorist refuses to participate in field sobriety testing.

The law concerning DUI cases involving alcohol is still the same and motorists may refuse field sobriety testing without consequence to their driving privileges. However, refusal of chemical testing, whether it involves a DUI based on alcohol or cannabis will still lead to a suspension in driving privileges.

Additionally, if a driver refuses chemical testing, the police officer may then seek to obtain a search warrant to allow for blood, urine, or saliva to be collected from the motorist. To do this, the officer must contact a judge, offer all the evidence that has been collected to that point, and if the judge determines that probable cause exists, then the judge will sign the warrant to allow the officer to collect the requested chemical sample. Should the motorist refuse to comply with the search warrant, they could possibly face felony obstruction charges.

DUI CANNABIS – LEGISLATIVE CHANGES AND ADDITIONAL SOBRIETY TESTS

In Illinois, the legalization of cannabis has brought about new challenges related to driving under the influence (DUI). For instance, with alcohol based DUIs, officers carry a portable breathalyzer that can give an assessment of a driver's BAC while at the scene of a traffic stop prior to any arrests. While there are similar technologies under development for the detection of cannabis levels, they are not widely available to officers in the field. This means that all chemical testing to determine the THC levels is done at a hospital and usually comes in the form of a blood draw, even though the law does provide for the detection of THC levels in other bodily fluids such as saliva and urine. This is likely why the legislature has decided to suspend the driving privileges for motorists that refuse field sobriety testing when they are suspected of being under the influence of cannabis.

While the traditional field sobriety tests were developed by the National Highway Traffic Safety Administration (NHTSA) to detect persons who were impaired by alcohol, the Illinois legislature has decided that these tests are also sufficient for persons who are suspected of being impaired by Cannabis. In practice, this is not always accurate. During their testing, NHTSA developed a battery of 3 tests that officers are trained on which include: the horizontal gaze nystagmus (HGN) test, the walk and turn test, and the one leg stand test. It should be noted that a person who is under the influence of cannabis will not exhibit any clues on the HGN test if it is conducted properly.

In addition to the standard tests, some officers have received advanced training on additional tests that were designed specifically for determining if someone is under the influence of cannabis or other drugs. There are two types of training programs that officers may receive. The first is the Advanced Roadside Impaired Driving Enforcement (ARIDE) which is a 16 hour classroom course. The second is a more intensive 40 hour course for an officer to become a drug recognition examiner (DRE) that actually teaches additional field sobriety tests exclusively for determining if a person is under the influence of drugs or cannabis. These tests include the modified romberg test and the lack of convergence test.

Modified Romberg Test

During the modified romberg test, the driver is instructed to stand with their feet together, arms at their sides, eyes closed, and head tilted up. The officer then asks the driver to estimate the passage of 30 seconds. After the passage of 30 seconds, the driver is then told to open his eyes and look toward the officer. During this test, the officer is looking for 3 different indicators: swaying, eye or body tremors, and time estimation. The theory being if a motorist is under the influence of cannabis, they would count slower and estimate a time much longer than 30 seconds. While motorists under the influence of cocaine or methamphetamines would estimate a time much shorter than 30 seconds.

Lack of Convergence Test

The lack of convergence test is the inability of an individual to cross their eyes when focusing on a stimulus as it is moved towards the bridge of their nose. The test is conducted by requiring a subject to follow a stimulus in a circle around the subject's face and then slowly moves the stimulus to within 2 inches of the subject's nose. If the subject's eyes do not cross when the stimulus is close to the bridge of the nose, then this is considered a sign of impairment.

While these tests are developed to detect drug impairment, they are extremely subjective and prone to officer error. It is often times the case that police officers will note clues of impairment that may not actually be present. In such cases, if a motorist elects to participate in these tests, they may still have their license suspended should the officer erroneously observe clues.

CHAPTER 11

DUI CHECKPOINTS

Most drivers, at some point in their life, have driven through some form of a police checkpoint. Checkpoints can be set up for a variety of reasons depending on the law enforcement goals, which typically include: Detection of impaired drivers, seatbelt checks, license checks, etc. The common setup for a checkpoint is to have one supervising officer directing traffic to different stations within the checkpoint. Each station would have a specific purpose and it is staffed with at least one officer. The usual stations include:

- **Pass through lane** – The lane where certain vehicles will be allowed to pass through the checkpoint without being screened
- **Primary screening area** – The area where officers will briefly stop the vehicle and ask for license/insurance and make a quick determination about whether the vehicle should be detained for further screening
- **Secondary screening area** – where more extensive investigations are done. This usually includes the

administration of field sobriety testing and additional questioning of the motorist

The majority of checkpoints are set up for the purpose of catching drunk drivers and are usually conducted in the late night or early morning hours when motorists are more likely to be intoxicated.

When setting up a checkpoint there are several things the police have to do to ensure that the random stopping of vehicles does not run afoul of the motorists' constitutional rights. The 4th amendment of the constitution provides that citizens should be free from unreasonable searches and seizures by the police. Even when initiating a traffic stop, a police officer must have probable cause to believe the driver committed a traffic violation prior to stopping that vehicle. Which begs the question, how can the police establish a checkpoint that randomly stops vehicles without probable cause and still pass constitutional muster?

The United States Supreme Court addressed this Issue when the Michigan State Police set up their first DUI checkpoint in 1986. Originally the case was thrown out at the State level as being a violation of the 4th amendment, however, the US Supreme Court reversed the ruling by saying that checkpoints can pass constitutional muster, as long as they comply with several requirements. Additionally, the Illinois Supreme Court has also ruled that DUI checkpoints are constitutional under certain circumstances, but requires the police to follow several well established protocols.

WHAT IS REQUIRED FOR THE POLICE TO SET UP A CHECKPOINT?

The courts apply a balancing test to determine whether a DUI checkpoint is constitutional. Should the State fall short in showing these factors, then the checkpoint can be ruled unconstitutional and any evidence collected as part of the checkpoint would be barred in court. Listed below are the 5 prongs Illinois Courts will look for when determining the constitutionality of a DUI roadblock.

- **The decision to establish the roadblock and the selection of the site are made by supervisory personnel**
    - The case law states that this must be a Sheriff, State Police Lieutenant, or Captain
    - This prong is not satisfied when these politically accountable persons delegate the roadblock to a subordinate. The official must be involved with the planning and design of the roadblock
- **The method employed to stop the vehicles is preestablished and systematic**
    - There must be an operations meeting with documentation that establishes the method for which vehicles will be stopped
    - The usual methods are 1 in 3 cars or 1 in 5 cars
    - It is not systematic for the police just pull cars over until the screening lane is full, or if the selection is left at the unbridled discretion of the site supervisor
- **The roadblock is operated in accordance with preexisting guidelines**
    - The guidelines must be reduced to writing and created by a politically accountable official
    - The guidelines must be distributed to all officers working the roadblock in an operations meeting

- **The official nature of the operation is sufficiently apparent and it is obvious that the roadblock does not, in fact, pose a safety risk**
- **The police's intent to establish the roadblock is publicized in advance**
    - This usually involves a brief blurb in a local paper
    - Social media post on department social media platforms usually do not satisfy this requirement

If the State falls short on these elements, then it is likely that the evidence may be suppressed and the arrest can be quashed. Amazingly, it is often the case that the majority of checkpoints do not adhere to these strict standards promulgated by the Supreme Court. An attorney that is familiar with roadblock litigation would be able to take advantage of this and be able to file a motion to suppress evidence and quash arrest that could possibly lead to a dismissal of any charge that resulted from the unconstitutional roadblock.

CHAPTER 12

CAN I GET A DUI IN A SELF DRIVING CAR?

The proliferation of self-driving technology has started to raise some very interesting legal questions. For instance, can a person get a DUI in a self driving car? What about traffic tickets? If the car is in control, am I responsible for its actions? Do I need a license to operate a self-driving vehicle? Currently, state legislative bodies have been slow to react to this paradigm shift in transportation, but we expect the laws to accommodate this newly available technology in the near future.

FULL SELF DRIVING HISTORY

Tesla has been working on self-driving technology for quite a while and other automakers have followed suit by providing their own versions of autonomous and semi-autonomous driving features. Back in 2019, Elon Musk made the claim that by 2020 their vehicles would be fully autonomous to the point that there would be a fleet of fully self-driving robotaxis that would require no human intervention. Since that statement four years ago, the development of fully autonomous vehicles has sputtered and there has even been a recall of Tesla vehicles equipped with the beta version of full self driving (FSD). The National Highway Traffic Safety Administration (NHTSA) released a statement indicating that it had concerns about the technology saying that the vehicles using the FSD System did not adequately adhere to safety laws and could cause crashes. Specifically, NHTSA claims that the software allows a vehicle to "exceed speed limits or travel through intersections in an unlawful or unpredictable manner and increases the risk of a crash."

In addition to the concerns from national regulators, there have been several instances where drivers were either asleep or were otherwise unresponsive while operating their vehicle. Currently, any version of autonomous driving technology is supposed to have safeguards that ensure the driver is engaged and monitoring driving conditions and vehicle actions. Most automakers have implemented a system that requires slight pressure to be applied to the steering wheel while the vehicle is in autonomous driving mode. This safeguard, however, has been defeated by several drivers by either placing objects on the wheel that will apply a slight tension, or a sleeping driver with their hand dangling from the wheel. There have been several instances of Tesla drivers asleep at the wheel while their vehicles were in motion. For instance, in September of 2021, police had to get in front of a Tesla vehicle to stop it when the driver was under the influence of alcohol and asleep at the wheel. Most recently, there were reports of a driver asleep while operating her Tesla on the interstate and several passing motorists tried honking their horn in an attempt to wake the driver. Because of this, Tesla and other car companies have started installing cameras within the vehicle that will track the driver's eyes and determine whether the driver is engaged with the road or distracted.

Despite these concerns, Elon Musk has doubled down on his robotaxi comments by saying Tesla will begin mass production of a fully autonomous vehicle, that is not equipped with a steering wheel or pedals, by 2024. Additionally, once full self driving exits the beta stage, there is talk that Tesla owners will be able to earn extra income by putting their car in robotaxi mode and have it perform ride-share services when they are not using it.

THE CURRENT STATE OF DUI AND TRAFFIC LAWS IN ILLINOIS

In Illinois, it is currently illegal to operate a motor vehicle while under the influence of drugs or alcohol, regardless of whether the vehicle is being driven manually or through autonomous technology.

While self-driving cars are equipped with advanced technology that allows them to operate without direct human input, they still require a human operator to monitor the vehicle's performance and intervene if necessary. Therefore, if you are in a self-driving car and you are impaired by drugs or alcohol to the extent that you are unable to take control of the vehicle if necessary, you could potentially be charged with a DUI in Illinois.

The traffic laws in Illinois are extremely strict, especially when it comes to driving under the influence. As the law currently stands, it is illegal to be in "actual physical control" of a vehicle anywhere in the state while you are impaired by drugs or alcohol. The phrase "actual physical control" has come to be broadly interpreted to mean anytime you're in a car and the keys are nearby. For instance, the appellate court affirmed a DUI conviction of a motorist that was parked on the side of the road, asleep in the backseat of his car, zipped in a sleeping bag, while the keys were laying on the rear floorboard.

Additionally, if you are behind the wheel of an autonomous vehicle, you will still be required to have valid driving privileges and obey all traffic laws. It is not a defense to say that the vehicle was in control during a particular infraction.

It is worth noting, however, that the laws and regulations surrounding autonomous vehicles are still evolving, and it is possible that they may change in the future to account for the unique challenges posed by these vehicles. It will be interesting to see, if and when Tesla actually puts out a fully autonomous vehicle that is not equipped with a steering wheel or pedals, how the legislature and appellate courts will adapt. In my opinion, it would be difficult to make an argument of "actual physical control" when there is no way for a driver to have specific control of a vehicle, other than to input a destination and enjoy the ride.

CHAPTER 13

EFFECTIVE DUI DEFENSES

In Illinois, DUI is a serious criminal offense. With it come all the protections afforded under the law. Being arrested or charged does not mean that you are automatically convicted and there are several defenses available to a DUI charge, which include:

- The police officer did not have a legally justifiable reason for stopping you
- The police established an illegal roadblock before pulling you over
- The breathalyzer was not calibrated properly
- The records for the breathalyzer were not properly kept
- The police officer did not have probable cause to believe you were under the influence of alcohol

Before presenting any of these defenses, you will first want to collect some information about the case. This usually involves filing a motion for discovery with the court. This will tell the prosecution that they must turn over all the information, including exculpatory information, that is related to the case. This usually includes police reports, witness statements, squad videos, body cameras (where available), calibration information for the breathalyzer (if one was used), and certification information for the officer that administered the breathalyzer. Once you have received this information, then you are ready to start building a defense for your case.

CHALLENGING THE STOP

The Fourth Amendment to the US constitution prevents police from being able to stop a motorist unless they have a good reason for doing so. There are several valid reasons that police effectuate traffic stops. These usually include: the police officer witnessed a violation of the Illinois Vehicle Code, the officer has received verifiable information that a person has committed a crime, or the police officer knows the driver to have a warrant for his arrest. Usually, police officers will document the basis of a traffic stop in their police report. For instance, a police officer may say he stopped a motorist for crossing the center line. If you are going to attack this assertion by the officer, you can do so by watching the video from the officer's squad and seeing if the vehicle actually crossed the center line. If in fact the vehicle never crossed the center line and there were no other violations of the Illinois Vehicle Code, then the next step would be to file a Motion to Suppress Evidence and set the case for a hearing. If the vehicle merely touches the center line and does not cross all the way over, this is usually not enough to justify an officer stopping a vehicle. At hearing, you would need to present the video to the court showing that no traffic violations occurred and therefore it was improper for the police officer to initiate a traffic stop.

CHALLENGING THE ARREST

Before police can arrest a driver for DUI, they must first gather enough evidence to establish "probable cause" for the arrest. If a police officer arrests someone prior to gathering that evidence, this would be considered an illegal detention pursuant to the fourth amendment and all evidence obtained as a result of that illegal detention will be suppressed and the arrest will be quashed.

When gathering evidence to establish probable cause, police officers look at the totality of the circumstances that go beyond the results of field sobriety testing. Police will consider several factors when making an arrest decision including a person's driving and behavior. Below is a list of things police usually include as evidence when establishing probable cause for a DUI arrest that are observed outside the administration of field sobriety testing.

- Driving prior to being pulled over
  - Weaving
  - Crossing the Center line or fog line
  - Varying speed
  - Disobeying traffic control devices
- Driver's demeanor when interacting with officers
  - Combative
  - Excited
  - Indifferent
  - Insulting
  - Using Profanity
  - Sleepy
- Balance
  - Falling
  - Hesitant

- Needing Support
- Staggering
- Unsteady
- Odor of alcohol on person/breath
  - Faint
  - Moderate
  - Strong
- Eyes
  - Bloodshot
  - Glassy
  - Droopy eye lids
  - Constricted
  - Dialated
- Speech
  - Mumbled
  - Slurred
  - Thick-tongued
- Unusual Actions
  - Belching
  - Vomiting
  - Hiccupping
  - Laughing
  - Fighting
  - Crying
- Portable Breathalyzer Test

Another thing to consider when challenging the probable cause for an arrest is trying to determine the moment in time when the driver was legally placed under arrest. Remember, the courts will look at how much evidence the officer has when a driver is placed under arrest when deciding a motion to suppress evidence. Everything that happens after the arrest, such as a certified breathalyzer result, will not be considered. A lot of times an officer will say something like "I'm placing you in handcuffs but you are not under arrest." Even though an officer may communicate to a person they are not under arrest, the court will look at all the circumstances involved when determining whether a person has been seized pursuant to the 4th amendment. Many courts all across the country continue to battle with this issue and there are many factors to consider in determining when a person is legally under arrest. Usually (but not always) when a person is in the back of a squad car in handcuffs, they are under arrest.

CHALLENGING BREATHALYZER RESULTS

In order for the prosecution to present a breathalyzer result at trial, they need to provide the appropriate foundation before the court will accept it. In order to do so, they need to present evidence that the certified breathalyzer was calibrated properly and that the officer administering the test had a current certification to operate the breathalyzer. Breathalyzer logs and officer certification information are usually obtained through filing a motion for discovery. If the prosecutor does not want to turn this information over, then it might be necessary to submit a subpoena to the police department in order to obtain this information.

The calibration and maintenance procedures for certified breathalyzers are contained in the Illinois Administrative Code. Section 1286.200 provides that a breathalyzer must meet all of the following to be presumed accurate at the time the test is given.

The procedures contained in this Subpart are the only procedures for establishing the accuracy of breath testing instruments. A rebuttable presumption exists that an instrument was accurate at the particular time a subject test was performed when the following four conditions are met.

a) *The instrument was approved under this Subpart at the time of the test.*
b) *The performance of the instrument was within the accuracy tolerance described in this Subpart according to the last accuracy check or verification (whichever is later) prior to the subject test.*
c) *No accuracy check has been performed subsequent to the subject test or the performance of the instrument on the next accuracy check after the subject test was within the accuracy tolerance described in this Subpart.*
d) *Accuracy checks have been done in a timely manner, meaning not more than 62 days have passed since the last accuracy check prior to the subject test;*

In addition to Section 1286.200, the state must also comply with Section 1286.230 listed below:

To ensure the continued accuracy of approved evidentiary instruments, a BAT or automated system shall perform accuracy checks.

a) *Checks shall be performed at least once every 62 days.*
b) *Checks shall consist of at least two tests of the instrument in which the instrument quantitates a reference sample.*
c) *Approved evidentiary instruments must quantitate a reference sample within 10 percent of the reference sample's value, as adjusted for environmental factors.*
d) *The accuracy check results shall be recorded in the instrument's logbook or internal memory, or in the central*

repository. The automatic accuracy checks or accuracy checks performed remotely will not be entered in the logbook. If the accuracy check was performed by a BAT at the instrument location, the accuracy check results shall be recorded in the instrument's logbook.

e) *The Director or his/her designee, at his/her discretion, may remove any approved evidential instrument located in any department, agency, or sheriff's office from active service due to lack of use.*

While Section 1286.200 indicates *"No accuracy check has been performed subsequent to the subject test"* Section 1286.230 requires accuracy checks be conducted at least once every 62 days. Meaning, if the subject test was done within 62 days of the previous calibration, if the subsequent calibration was performed more than 62 days after the initial calibration, then there is a presumption of unreliability.

Essentially, the breathalyzer will need to be checked for accuracy every 62 days in order for the courts to recognize it as accurate. In the past, it has happened that the police department upgraded its breathalyzer equipment and forgot to run an accuracy check prior to disposing of the old breathalyzer. This meant that all results between the upgrade and the last calibration of the unit were not per-se accurate pursuant to the administrative code. Remember, there must be a calibration check before AND after the breathalyzer test for the courts to consider this compliant with the administrative code. Consider the following hypothetical. The police department certifies a breathalyzer as accurate on July 1. A driver submits to a breathalyzer test on July 2. The next accuracy check is not completed until September 15. The test that was submitted to on July 2 would not be considered accurate pursuant to the administrative code, even though the test was conducted just one day after the CBT was certified as accurate. This is because more than 62 days passed since the accuracy check on July 1 and the one on September 15. Therefore, all the tests given between July 1 and September 15 will be in violation of the administrative code and the results will not be presumed to be accurate in the eyes of the court.

On a side note, I recently had an officer read a previous version of my book and challenge my assertion that the results could be suppressed if the breathalyzer was not calibrated within 62 days. His understanding was if a subject submitted to a breathalyzer result and there was a calibration at least 62 days prior to the test, then that calibration would be considered accurate, irrelevant of when the next calibration occurred. However, there is specific case law in People v. Clairmont 961 N.E.2d 914 that requires calibrations before and after the subject test and that those calibrations need to be within 62 days of each other. The Clairmont case involved 2 defendants trying to suppress the certified breathalyzer based on the state not adhering to the 62 day calibration standard. The first defendant was tested 60 days after the initial calibration and the second calibration was 11 days after the defendant's test, totaling 71 days between the two calibrations. The second defendant was tested 3 days after the initial calibration and the second calibration was not done until 62 days after the defendant's test, totaling 65 days between calibrations. The court held the breathalyzer results inadmissible based on their non-compliance with section 1286.230 of title 20 of the Administrative Code. The court did, however, note that the lack of strict compliance with the code did not automatically render the results inadmissible. Instead, it merely created a presumption of unreliability and allows for the State to present further evidence of substantial compliance to rebut the presumption of unreliability. The court did not opine on what it would consider "substantial compliance".

The Portable breathalyzer (PBT), while not admissible at trial, still has to be calibrated pursuant to the administrative code. These standards, however, are not as rigorous as the standards for the certified breathalyzer and only require accuracy checks every 93 days. Even though PBT results are not admissible at trial, it is sometimes beneficial to try and exclude the result of a PBT when arguing a motion to quash arrest or suppress evidence (where PBT results are admissible). Often times when the police make a DUI arrest, the primary evidence that they use to support probable cause for the arrest will be the PBT result. If the PBT result is ruled inadmissible, then the courts may find that there was not enough evidence to support the arrest and all evidence will be suppressed, which can lead to a dismissal of the charges. While the certified breathalyzer will almost always be calibrated in a timely manner, it is often that case that officers will allow their PBTs to go past the calibration dates. This is most likely because the PBT is carried around in the squad car with the officer, while the certified breathalyzer resides at the police station.

Another way to suppress the PBT is to alleged that the officer did not request the driver to take the test and instead tried to force it upon him. The code indicates that an officer, once they have reasonable suspicion that a person committed a DUI *"may request the person to provide a sample of his or her breath for a preliminary breath screening test"*. The "may request" language means that the PBT has to be offered to the driver. If the officer simply tells the driver to take the test, this would violate the statute and the PBT result could be suppressed.

KNOW YOUR RIGHTS WHEN STOPPED BY LAW ENFORCEMENT

When you are stopped for DUI or any other traffic offense, you have several rights guaranteed to you by our judicial system including the right to remain silent. You are not required to answer any questions or participate in field sobriety testing. Often times, police officers will try to bolster the case against you by asking about where you are going, where you are coming from or how much you had to drink. It's important to remember that anything you say during this encounter with the police may be used against you at a hearing or trial.

WHAT ARE NO REFUSAL WEEKENDS?

A lot of times, law enforcement will work with the State's Attorney's Office to sponsor what's called a "No Refusal Weekend". Basically, what happens is a group of Judges that are willing to work during the weekend and stay up until 3 am, will be on call to sign search warrants for DUI cases. These search warrants allow for chemical testing of motorists who are suspected of Driving Under the Influence. When an officer stops a motorist and suspects they are driving under the influence, that officer will radio the on-call judge, present her with all the circumstances surrounding a DUI arrest and if the Judge finds probable cause to exist for a DUI charge, then she will sign a search warrant allowing the arresting officer to perform chemical testing. If the motorist then refuses chemical testing in the face of a search warrant, that motorist will be charged with Obstruction, a Class 4 Felony. While the laws in Illinois allow for a motorist to refuse chemical testing, they do not allow a motorist to refuse in the face of a search warrant signed by a judge.

CHAPTER 14

POSSIBLE WAYS TO RESOLVE A DUI CASE

How you choose to resolve your DUI can have a significant impact on your life and driving privileges. In addition to any criminal penalties, such as jail time and fines, there may also be collateral consequences to your plea that may involve a revocation of your license. If you are convicted of DUI in Illinois, even on your first offense, your license will be revoked. This revocation will be in addition to any license suspension that you may have received for failing or refusing chemical testing. There are only a limited number of ways that a DUI can be resolved.

PLEA BARGAIN

The most common way a DUI case is resolved is by reaching an agreement with the State's Attorney's Office. A plea bargain may include an amended charge, a reduced charge, or an offer of court supervision which will lead to a dismissal once the supervision is completed. This may also result in the dismissal of any companion charges such as speeding or improper lane use. Additionally, it is also possible to reach an agreement on your pending license suspension. If you filed a timely petition to rescind statutory summary suspension, it is possible for the prosecutor to agree to your petition as part of the plea agreement.

Once a plea agreement has been reached, it still needs to be accepted by the court. This is done in open court. The parties recite the terms of the agreement, and the court can either accept or reject the terms. If the court rejects the terms, then the parties can either renegotiate the agreement or the case may be set for trial.

OPEN PLEA

If the prosecutor is not willing to offer acceptable terms in exchange for a plea of guilty, then you may have the court impose a sentence for the charge. This is usually referred to as an open plea or a blind plea. Because there is no agreement being presented, it will be left up to the judge to determine the appropriate sentence.

It is possible for the prosecutor to dismiss companion charges in exchange for an open plea. Usually a prosecutor will dismiss the petty companion tickets in exchange for a plea to the DUI, then it will be up to the Judge to determine an appropriate sentence for the DUI.

The prosecutor may even be willing to offer a "cap" on the sentencing. For instance, the prosecutor may say that he will not ask for more than 30 days in jail in exchange for a plea of guilty. The court, however, is not bound by the prosecutor's cap. While rare, it is possible for a court to enter a sentence that is above the cap recommended by the prosecutor.

402 CONFERENCE

A 402 conference is a special conference that gets the Judge involved in negotiations for a case. If the defense and the prosecutor are unable to reach an agreement, then it is possible to ask the Judge what the sentence will most likely be if you were to open plea the case. This conference is conducted in the Judge's chambers and is attended by the Defense Attorney, the Prosecutor, and the Judge. Both the prosecution and the defense must agree to this conference before it can take place. You are not legally entitled to have a 402 conference, and if the prosecutor does not agree to it, then it will not take place.

If possible, it is always advisable to conduct a 402 conference prior to an open plea, so you can understand what the sentence will likely be prior to a sentencing hearing. During this conference, the Judge will recommend a sentence that may be better than what the state is offering. It is also possible, however, that the judge will recommend a sentence that is above what the State is asking for. Its important to know that after this conference, you are not required to accept the Judge's recommendation. You may reject the recommendation and continue negotiating with the prosecutor or set your case for trial.

DISMISSAL

If the prosecutor concedes that the evidence against you is not sufficient, they may choose to dismiss your case. While this is possible, it is rare. Usually, a dismissal will come after the defense attorney has successfully argued a motion to quash arrest or suppress evidence. Once the arrest has been quashed and evidenced suppressed, the prosecution will be limited in what they can present at trial and their hand will be forced to dismiss the case.

NOT GUILTY VERDICT

If your case is taken to trial, and the prosecutor is unable to present sufficient evidence for the jury or the judge to find you guilty beyond a reasonable doubt, then a not guilty verdict will enter. Once you are found not guilty, you will not be subject to any of the fines or penalties that are associated with the case, and you will be eligible to have the case expunged from your record.

GUILTY VERDICT

If your case is taken to trial and the prosecutor convinces the jury that you are guilty beyond a reasonable doubt, then the judgment of conviction will enter against you and it will be up to the Judge to determine an appropriate sentence. The case will be set out for a sentencing hearing whereby you are allowed to present evidence to the court to ask for a lesser sentence. The prosecution will also be given the opportunity to present evidence and can make recommendations to the court on what they think an appropriate sentence should be.

CHAPTER 15

DUI FAQ

WILL MY LICENSE BE SUSPENDED IF I GET A DUI?

Illinois is an "Implied Consent" State and all persons using the public highways are said to have given their consent to submit to chemical testing upon the request of law enforcement. If you refuse a breathalyzer or fail testing, then your license will be suspended.

HOW DO I GET MY LICENSE BACK AFTER A DUI SUSPENSION?

Just because the suspension period is over does not mean your driver's license is automatically valid. You must contact the Illinois Secretary of State and pay a reinstatement fee before they lift the suspension on your license. It is recommended that you pay this fee approximately one month prior to the termination of your suspension to ensure that your license is valid once the suspension has terminated. You may check the status of your driving privileges by using the Secretary of State's automatic phone system at (217) 785-8619.

HOW LONG WILL MY LICENSE BE SUSPENDED?

IF YOU FAILED CHEMICAL TESTING

- Six month suspension if you have not had a DUI in the last 5 years
- One year suspension if your last DUI was within the last 5 years

IF YOU REFUSED CHEMICAL TESTING

- One year suspension if you have not had a DUI in the last 5 years
- 3 year suspension if your last DUI was within the last 5 years

HOW DO I GET MY LICENSE BACK AFTER A DUI REVOCATION?

If your license is revoked for a DUI, you will need to have a hearing before a Secretary of State hearing officer before regaining driving privileges. This is often an onerous and expensive process that usually involves not having driving privileges for a substantial period of time.

WHAT IS THE DIFFERENCE BETWEEN A LICENSE SUSPENSION AND REVOCATION?

A license suspension is for a predetermined amount of time. Upon the expiration of the suspension, the driver must simply pay the reinstatement fee to become valid. A revocation is an indefinite removal of driving privileges. If a driver is revoked, they must have a hearing before a Secretary of State Hearing Officer and be approved before they may regain driving privileges.

AM I ELIGIBLE FOR A PERMIT?

For offenders who had their license suspended because they refused or failed chemical testing AND have not had a DUI within the last 5 years may apply for a MDDP (Monitoring Device Driving Permit) to have driving privileges during the period of suspension. This permit allows you to drive anytime and anywhere as long as you operate a vehicle that is Equipped with a BAIID (Breath Alcohol Ignition Interlock Device). This device requires the driver to submit a breath sample prior to starting their car. The car will only start if the driver has no alcohol in their system. To apply for this permit, you will need to submit a MDDP application to the Secretary of State's Office. This application will be mailed to you once the Secretary of State has confirmed the suspension on your license. If you do not receive the application, you may download it from the Secretary of State's website at https://www.ilsos.gov/publications/pdf_publications/baiid24.pdf

WHAT IS A FIELD SOBRIETY TEST SUSPENSION

A Field Sobriety Test Suspension only applies to DUI Cannabis Cases. If an officer has reasonable suspicion to believe a driver is impaired by cannabis, and that driver fails or refuses to participate in field sobriety testing, then their license will be suspended. It is important to know that a person whose license is suspended through a field sobriety test suspension will not be eligible for a Monitoring Device Driving Permit (MDDP).

CAN I FIGHT THE SUSPENSION OF MY LICENSE?

Yes. You may file a petition to rescind the suspension on your license with the Circuit Court within 90 days of when you were given notice of the suspension. After filing this petition, the petitioner is given an opportunity to present legal proof to the court to have the suspension rescinded. If the court believes that police officers did not have probable cause to initiate a traffic stop or effectuate a DUI arrest, or there is a technical defect in the paperwork or breath results, you might have the suspension of your license rescinded.

DO I HAVE TO TAKE A BREATHALYZER?

Unless you were involved in an accident involving death or great bodily injury to another person, you may refuse a breathalyzer or chemical testing. If you refuse, however, your driver's license may be subject to a statutory summary suspension. Under Illinois law, the police can only demand that you take a breathalyzer or submit to chemical testing if they have enough probable cause to believe you were driving under the influence. Prior to administering any breathalyzer or chemical testing, police are required to read you warnings listing the consequences of failing or refusing the test. If you refuse a breathalyzer, the officer may then get a search warrant, which needs to be signed by a judge, that requires you to submit to chemical testing. If you refuse chemical testing in the face of a search warrant, then you will be charged with a class 4 felony of obstruction.

WHAT ARE FIELD SOBRIETY TESTS?

When a police officer initiates a traffic stop and suspects that the driver is impaired, he may ask that the driver complete a series of sobriety tests. There are three standard field sobriety test that the National Highway Traffic Safety Administration (NHTSA) has developed that police officers use to determine if someone is under the influence of alcohol. These are the Horizontal Gaze Nystagmus Test (HGN), walk and turn test and one leg stand test. During the HGN test, an officer will have the subject follow his finger while he looks for nystagmus (slight shaking) in the subjects eyes. The walk and turn test involves the subject taking 9 heel-to-toe steps on a line, executing a turn and taking 9 steps back. During the one leg stand test, the subject is required to raise one foot 6 inches off the ground for 30 seconds while keeping their hands by their side. During these test, police officers look "clues" that are defined by NHTSA.

WHAT ARE NON-STANDARD FIELD SOBRIETY TESTS?

Sometimes officers will try to administer sobriety test that are not certified by the National Highway Traffic Safety Administration (NHTSA). Some of these test include alphabet test, number test, and finger to nose test. These test are usually administered by conservation officers who may not have access to a flat, dry surface required for conducting the standard field sobriety tests. Since these tests are not certified by NHTSA, their results may not be legally admissible.

DO I HAVE TO DO FIELD SOBRIETY TESTING?

You are not required to participate in any field sobriety testing. Often times these tests are not conducted in an environment that is ideal for administering these tests. The National Highway Traffic Safety Administration (NHTSA) requires these test to be conducted in an area with a hard, smooth , flat, dry surface. Usually, police officers will make the subject perform these tests on the side of the road at night while traffic is passing despite the regulations promulgated by NHTSA. However, if an officer has a reasonable belief that the driver is under the influence of cannabis, then it might be possible for your license to become suspended should you refuse to participate in field sobriety tests.

IF I BLOW UNDER THE LIMIT, WILL MY CASE BE DISMISSED?

Not necessarily. Illinois DUI laws strongly favor the prosecution of impaired drivers and the State's Attorney's Office may still bring charges against you even if your BAC was below .08. The law states that there is a presumption of impairment when a driver's BAC is over .08. If the BAC was less than .05 then there is a presumption that the driver was not under the influence of alcohol. If a driver's BAC is greater than .05 but less than .08 then there is no presumption and the prosecution may present additional evidence of driver impairment to convict a driver of DUI.

IF THE POLICE DO NOT READ MY RIGHTS, WILL MY CASE BE DISMISSED?

Not necessarily. Police are only required to advise a person of their Miranda rights only after a person is placed under arrest, or their freedom is so severely hindered that a reasonable person would believe they were in police custody. If a Police Officer interrogates you while you are in custody and your statements are a significant part of the evidence against you, the fact that Miranda was not read could result in those statements not being allowed as evidence in your case. This could result in a dismissal, reduction in charges or a not-guilty verdict at trial.

GLOSSARY

402 conference – A 402 conference is governed by Illinois Supreme Court Rule 402. Essentially if the parties are unable to come to agreeable terms to resolve a pending case, they may ask the judge to get involved in negotiations. Both parties must agree to conduct a 402 conference before it may take place. Attendance in a 402 conference is limited to the Defense attorney, the prosecutor and the judge. The Defendant and the alleged victim will not be allowed to attend. During the conference, the attorneys do not have to follow the rules of evidence and the Judge may hear facts about the Defendant and the alleged victim that are not admissible at a trial or a hearing. The judge will make a recommendation about what sentence might be should the Defendant open plea to the charges. Either party is free to reject the recommendation of the judge. Conducting a 402 conference does not obligate the Defendant to plead guilty and the Defendant may still have a trial.

Bench Trial – A lawful proceeding in Illinois whereby a judge, not a jury, makes a determination as to the defendant's guilt or innocence. If a defendant wishes to take their case to trial, they must decide whether they want a trial by jury or trial by judge. The defendant is the only person that can decide what type of trial to have in their case. The judge, the prosecutor, and even the defendant's attorney cannot force the defendant to choose one type of trial over the other. Prior to setting a bench trial, the defendant must make a knowing and voluntary waiver of trial by jury.

Blind Plea – See open plea

Bond Conditions – With the elimination of cash bond in Illinois pursuant to the Pretrial Fairness portion of Safe-T Act the majority of DUI cases are considered "non-detainable" offenses. Which means that pretrial release will be guaranteed. However, the court may still place conditions upon an individual's release that must be followed while the case is pending. The law states that these conditions must be the least restrictive means possible and must be individualized.

Breath Alcohol Interlock Ignition Device (BAIID) – This is a device that attaches to a vehicle's ignition system and requires the driver to blow into it before the vehicle is able to start. If the Device detects the driver's BAC to be above .025 then the vehicle will not start. Additionally, the driver will be asked periodically during their drive to pull over and reblow into the device.

Detainable Offense – These are offenses that are eligible for the State to file a motion to hold the defendant in custody prior to trial. These offenses include non-probationable felonies, forcible felonies, stalking, violation of an order of protection, domestic battery, etc. If the State files a motion to detain a defendant, they must prove by clear and convincing evidence that the defendant is a danger to the public or a particular person, and there are no set of bond conditions that can mitigate that danger.

Expert Witness – A witness that is allowed to offer his or her opinion at trial about a particular aspect of the case for which they are uniquely qualified. Usually, courts prohibit witnesses from offering their opinions as testimony. However, if it can be shown that a witness has necessary qualifications and experience within their field, the court may view that witness as an expert and allow the witness to opine about matters that are within their field of expertise. Generally speaking, experts may testify about their conclusions in a case so long as their analysis is scientifically sound. In reaching their conclusions, experts may rely on the same sorts of evidence that people in their profession normally rely on in their work, even if the evidence is otherwise inadmissible in court. For example, a doctor may testify about his analysis of X-rays, even though the X-rays would normally be considered hearsay.

Grand Jury - The Constitution and laws of Illinois provide that no person shall be brought to trial for a crime punishable by imprisonment in the penitentiary unless either the initial charge has been brought by indictment of a grand jury or the person has been given a prompt preliminary hearing and a judge has found probable cause. The grand jury is presented with evidence and is asked if probable cause exists for the state to proceed with felony charges. Should the grand jury find probable cause, then a bill of indictment is returned and tendered to the defendant. Unlike a jury for a criminal trial where the jury must be unanimous to convict a defendant, in an Illinois grand jury, only 9 jurors must agree for the State to proceed forward with felony charges against the defendant.

Hearsay - An out-of-court statement offered to prove the truth of matter asserted. Generally, hearsay evidence is not admissible at trial, but there are exceptions to the hearsay rule.

Jury Trial – A lawful proceeding in Illinois in which 12 members of the community make a determination as to the defendant's guilt or innocence. These 12 members are selected from a pool of approximately 50 potential jurors. The prosecution, the defense, and the court will be allowed to ask the potential jurors question to ensure they can be fair and impartial in rendering a verdict. The verdict must be unanimous among all 12 jurors. If the jury cannot come to a unanimous decision after extended deliberation, commonly referred to as a hung jury, then the court will dismiss the jury without returning a verdict. If no verdict is returned, the charges will still be pending against the defendant and the parties may renegotiate the case or reset the case for trial.

Monitoring Device Driving Permit (MDDP) – This is a permit that allows a person charged with a DUI, who is subject to a statutory summary suspension (SSS) to drive during the period of that suspension, assuming they have not had a DUI or SSS within the last 5 years. The permit will allow a person to drive anytime and anywhere as long as they operate a vehicle equipped with a BAIID.

Motion in Limine – This is a motion that is usually filed and ruled on prior to a jury trial. These motions may be filed by either the prosecution or defense and seek to limit the evidence and arguments the other side may present. The purpose of this motion is to prevent the interjection of irrelevant and inadmissible evidence that may be prejudicial.

Non-Detainable Offense – With the Pretrial Fairness act, criminal defendants are no longer required to post a cash bond. However, a person may still be held while their case is pending if their charge is considered detainable by statute, and the State proves by clear and convincing evidence that the defendant is a danger to the community or a specific identifiable person and there is no combination of bond conditions that can mitigate that danger. If a charge is considered non-detainable, then that person will be released while their case is pending and will remain out of custody, unless they violate the conditions of their release. The majority of DUI offenses are considered non-detainable offenses.

Open Plea – An open plea is sometimes referred to as a blind plea. This is when the defense and the prosecution are unable to reach a fully negotiated agreement and the defense is asking the judge to determine the appropriate sentence. After a defendant pleads guilty to the charge, the case will be set for a sentencing hearing where each side may call witnesses, present evidence, make arguments, and give the court recommendations about what they believe is an appropriate sentence. After hearing the evidence, the judge will determine the sentence. Sometimes open pleas can involve a partial agreement between the parties. For instance, the State may be willing to dismiss some of the companion charges or offer a cap on their recommendation to the judge should the defendant plead guilty. If a cap is part of the plea, its important to know that the judge is not bound by the recommendations of the cap and may go above the cap. While it is a rare situation for the judge to exceed the recommendations from the State, it does happen and it is something that the Defendant should be aware of prior to conducting an open plea with a cap.

Plea Bargain – During the pendency of a case, the defense and prosecution are free to negotiate terms to possibly resolve the case. These terms may involve an amended charge, a reduced charge, or a dismissal of companion charges. Should the parties come to an agreement, then they must present their agreement to the court for approval. If the court accepts the agreement, the case is resolved and the terms of the agreement become the order of the court. If the court rejects the agreement, the court may give guidance to the parties about how the agreement may be modified so it is acceptable to the court.

Pre-Sentence Investigation (PSI) – An investigation into the history of a defendant convicted of a crime. This is conducted prior to a sentencing hearing and is used to determine if there are any aggravating or mitigating factors about the defendant. This investigation is usually conducted by the probation department and includes an interview with the defendant. At the conclusion of the pre-sentence investigation, a PSI report will be forwarded to the prosecution, the defendant, and the court. This report will contain the results of the investigation which will include any statements the defendant made, the factual basis of the offense, information about the defendant's family members, living situation, work history, any treatment previously completed, criminal history, and anything else the investigating officer deems relevant to the proceeding.

Pretrial Conference – A pretrial conference is a court hearing that precedes trial. During this court appearance, the court will be looking for guidance from the parties to determine the status of the pending case. The parties will indicate whether they believe the case will be resolved with a plea or litigated at trial.

Pretrial Services – This department is responsible for collecting and analyzing information about a defendant used in determining risk. This department will also make recommendations to the court about what conditions should be placed upon a defendant for pretrial release. Pretrial services will also monitor defendant to ensure they are complying with all conditions of pretrial release including drug testing, participating in treatment, curfew requirements, etc.

Pretrial Services Report – This report is completed by the pretrial services department after a defendant is arrested. This report will contain information about the defendant's prior criminal history, living situation, brief information about the offense charged, and usually contains numerical scoring instruments that quantifies the potential risk to society should the defendant be released.

Restricted Driving Permit (RDP) – This is a permit similar to a MDDP in that the driver must operate a vehicle that is equipped with a BAIID. Additionally, the permit holder will be subject to restrictions on when, where, and for which purpose they may drive. An RDP holder will usually be able to drive to and from work, doctors visits, and treatment providers and they must provide a schedule to the Secretary of State verifying these times. A person must have a hearing with the Secretary of State in order to obtain an RDP and is usually only available to persons who have had their license revoked for DUI, or who have a statutory summary suspension and are not eligible for the MDDP.

Retrograde Extrapolation – This is a scientific technique that uses a defendant's blood alcohol concentration (BAC) obtained at a later time to estimate what their BAC was at an earlier time (usually when a defendant was driving). Experts, usually for the State, will usually base their opinion on the average rate at which alcohol is eliminated from the body. This is only admissible through expert testimony and case law and severely limited its use at trial because there are many unknown variables in the process, such has what a person had to eat, when they consumed alcohol, and if they were in-fact in the elimination stage instead of the absorption stage. It is possible for a person's BAC to continue to rise up to 2 hours after they last consumed alcohol, if they were to have consumed a substantial amount of fats and proteins prior to drinking.

Sentence Cap – At a sentencing hearing, both the defense and prosecution will make recommendations to the judge on what they believe is an appropriate sentence for the pending charges to which the defendant has either pled guilty or been found guilty. In certain circumstances, the prosecution may offer a cap on their recommendation. This is usually done in consideration of the defendant pleading guilty. When offering a cap, the prosecution is bound by their recommendation, but the judge is not. While rare, it is possible for the judge to enter a sentence that is above the cap recommended by the prosecutor.

Sentencing Hearing – A hearing that takes place after a defendant is found guilty at trial, or the defendant pleads guilty prior to trial without having an agreement with the prosecution (blind plea). At this hearing, both the prosecution and the defense will be given an opportunity to present evidence to the judge and make sentence recommendations for what they believe is an appropriate disposition for the pending charge. The defendant will be afforded an opportunity to make a statement in allocution after all the evidence is presented. At the conclusion of the hearing, the judge will sentence the defendant based on the evidence, recommendation of the parties, prior criminal history of the defendant, information contained in the pre-sentence report, the facts of the case, and the defendant's statement in allocution.

Statement in Allocution – A statement made by a defendant near the conclusion of a sentencing hearing. This is an opportunity for the defendant to address the court directly, without being subject to cross-examination. The defendant can inform the court about any special circumstances surrounding the offense and mention other factors in mitigation for the court to consider prior to passing sentence.

Statutory Summary Suspension – Illinois is an "implied consent" state, whereby every person operating on an Illinois highway has deemed to have given consent to take chemical testing when asked. Should an officer have probable cause to believe a person has committed a DUI on a public highway in Illinois and that person either refuses a breathalyzer or fails a breathalyzer test, then that person's license will be summarily suspended.

Statutory Summary Revocation – This is for DUI cases that involve great bodily harm or death. This is an administrative revocation that cannot be challenged in court and the only was to remove it from your license is to have a hearing with the Secretary of State.

Truth in Sentencing – A requirement whereby offenders convicted of an enumerated list of violent crimes are required to serve 75%, 85% or 100% of their sentence. Most offenses in Illinois only require offenders to serve 50% of their sentence.

Voir Dire - The process by which prospective jurors are questioned about their backgrounds and potential biases before being chosen to sit on a jury. During this process, the prosecution, the defense, and the judge may question potential jurors. If during the questioning it is determined that a potential juror cannot be fair and impartial, then the judge may remove that juror for cause. If either the prosecution or defense believe a potential juror would be detrimental to their side, and that juror is not subject to removal for cause, then they may remove that juror by using a challenge. Each side has a predetermined number of challenges that varies based on the severity of the offense. Either side may use a challenge at anytime during the voir dire process to remove a potential juror.

ABOUT THE AUTHOR

Illinois Criminal Defense Attorney Jonathan James has successfully represented hundreds of clients charged with DUI. He is a member of the Illinois State Bar Association and has received several awards including: The National Trial Lawyers "Top 100", The National Academy of Criminal Defense Attorneys "Top 10 Under 40", and the Lawyers of Distinction "Top 10% in the USA" in the area of criminal defense.

Mr. James graduated with a Bachelor of Science degree from Clemson University where he received several awards including Dean's List, President's List, and was a member of the Upsilon Pi Epsilon Honor Society. Mr. James attended Northern Illinois University College of Law where he graduated with a degree of Juris Doctor. Currently Mr. James runs The Law Office of Jonathan James, LLC, which has offices in Rockford, IL and Dekalb, IL.

For more information about his DUI Defense practice, visit his website at www.RockfordDUILaw.com. To schedule an appointment to speak with an experienced DUI defense attorney call our office at 779.500.0167